CRE▲TIVE
HOMEOWNER®

decorating
to go

DECORATING TO GO

SENIOR EDITOR Kathie Robitz
JUNIOR EDITOR Jennifer Calvert
GRAPHIC DESIGNER Kathryn Wityk
DIGITAL IMAGING SPECIALIST
    Frank Dyer
PHOTO COORDINATOR Mary Dolan
INDEXER Schroeder Indexing
    Services
FRONT & BACK COVER ILLUSTRATIONS
    Karen Wolcott
BACK COVER PHOTOGRAPHY
    (top) courtesy of IKEA;
    (bottom) courtsey of ORG

CREATIVE HOMEOWNER

VP AND PUBLISHER Timothy O. Bakke
ART DIRECTOR David Geer
MANAGING EDITOR Fran J. Donegan
PRODUCTION COORDINATOR
    Sara M. Markowitz

Current Printing (last digit)
10 9 8 7 6 5 4 3 2 1

Manufactured in the
United States of America

Decorating to Go, First Edition
Library of Congress
    Control Number: 2008943782
ISBN-10: 1-58011-458-X
ISBN-13: 978-1-58011-458-5

CREATIVE HOMEOWNER®
A Division of Federal Marketing Corp.
24 Park Way
Upper Saddle River, NJ 07458
www.creativehomeowner.com

Planet Friendly Publishing
✔ Made in the United States
✔ Printed on Recycled Paper
  Text: 10%   Cover: 10%
GREEN EDITION Learn more: www.greenedition.org

At Creative Homeowner we're committed to producing books in an earth-friendly manner and to helping our customers make greener choices.

Manufacturing books in the United States ensures compliance with strict environmental laws and eliminates the need for international freight shipping, a major contributor to global air pollution.

And printing on recycled paper helps minimize our consumption of trees, water, and fossil fuels. *Decorating to Go* was printed on paper made with 10% post-consumer waste. According to Environmental Defense's Paper Calculator, by using this innovative paper instead of conventional papers, we achieved the following environmental benefits:

Trees Saved: 20

Water Saved: 7,256 gallons

Solid Waste Eliminated: 1,204 pounds

Air Emissions Eliminated: 2,223 pounds

For more information on our environmental practices, please visit us online at www.creativehomeowner.com/green

36/3

dedication

For my incredibly wonderful, beautiful, and creative children,
Patrick, Gina, and Tessa, who fill my life with joy; for my sisters,
Stephanie and Pam, for their continual support in all my endeavors;
and for my beloved father, TGJL, who taught me how to improvise,
be creative, and plan ahead. —AN

For JL, who always made the right moves. —RB

acknowledgments

I want to especially thank Robin Bernard, for being an awesome mother,
mentor, and co-author; my husband, Pat, for all the hard work he does
daily so that the rest of us can do what we do. I also want to thank
Joanna Gavin and Jen Calvert for their help, thoughtfulness, support,
and feedback while working on this project. —AN

Many thanks to Jen, Kathryn, and Kathie for their skill and
guidance, and most of all to Adrienne, whose knowledge, creativity,
and loving patience made it all come together. —RB

contents

introduction

Spending decades in the same house is
pretty rare in our ever-changing society.
People upgrade, downsize, and find
themselves moving in, out, up, and on.
When you start out on your own, there's
the dorm, the first apartment, a town-
house, a starter home—and each temporary nest is like your own blank
canvas. The challenge, and the fun, is
to fill it with color, furnishings, and accessories that suit your
lifestyle, your budget, and your personality without making
"permanent" impressions. For example, knowing that you won't
be staying forever will probably rule out any major renovations, and you may
have a list of "don'ts" from your landlord. Those limiting factors can actually
inspire you to be more creative and find exciting ways to turn your new digs
into a warm and welcoming space. A big plus is that most of what you do
can be undone, packed up, and taken along for the next stop along the way.

Decorating to Go is designed
to be your friendly guide on
this challenging adventure.

chapter 1

Finding a Fit

When you slip on your favorite jeans or shoes, you know what a perfect fit feels like. You also know when you land a job you love or share a laugh with someone special. The odd thing is that a dwelling—whether it's a studio apartment or a penthouse—won't really feel like home until you're there a while and make all the little adjustments that will truly fit your needs and personality. It's that good-to-be-home feeling when you walk through your door, knowing what time the mail arrives, finding your way to the fridge in the dark, and greeting the neighbor's dog by name. That's when it occurs to you that instead of referring to "the apartment," you've started calling it "home."

Space Walk

Now that you've plunked down your money, signed the lease, and have the key, it's time to **take an unhurried walk-through and figure out the best way to use your new space.** Are there surprises? Did you discover that the closet in the nice, bright bedroom is only big enough to hold a lunchbox? Do you have a kitchen cabinet that's ideal for your dishes but leaves you wondering where you'll put the cereal? Where will your brother sleep when he visits? Where can you hide the litter box? Don't panic. Plan.

Make a Sketch

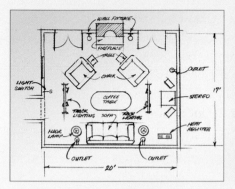
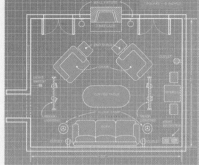

The best tools at this stage are a measuring tape and graph paper. As you draw the dimensions of each room, be sure to include the small things that can make a big difference: windows, doors, closets, radiators or heat registers, phone and cable jacks, baseboard heaters, exposed pipes, and built-in dividers or columns. (Don't just sketch them; really measure them.) It's also a good idea to take some "before" photos. They'll come in handy while you shop, and very handy when you're ready to move.

space walk

Quick Tip

You may not get more than one chance to see your new place before you move into it, so while you're there, take some snapshots—even if you just use your cell phone. It's a lot easier to refer to actual photos than mental pictures.

Make a List

Once you've measured, get comfy and make a list of furniture you already have and want to keep, as well as a wish list. Then let your fingers do the work. One option is buying a furniture placement kit. It comes with cutouts that can be moved around so that you can try different arrangements. **If you love doing everything on your computer, have fun playing with a 3-D room design program.** Any of these methods will work, but you'll be just fine with a sketch on paper as long as you know the room dimensions and square footage you have available for furniture and floor coverings.

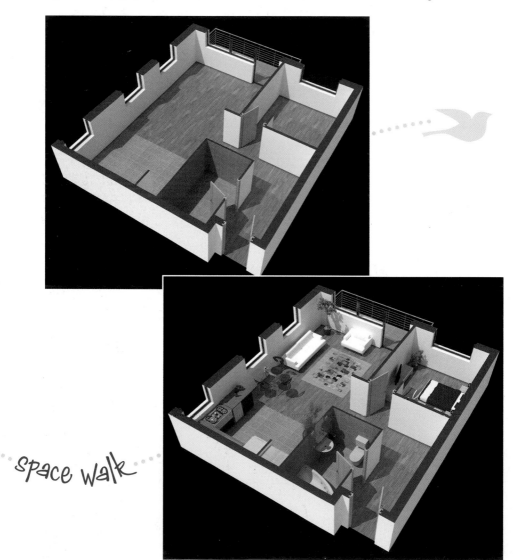

space walk

To Have & Have Not

When you go out to shop, make sure you take along the list of things you need and the sketch you drew. Then you'll be able to see at a glance whether there's actually enough space for everything. Is there room for a bed, or would it be better to look for a sofa bed? Will your old sectional fit, or should you split it up and store a third of it in Aunt Maggie's basement? Can you find room for the things that are most important to you? Is there enough space for a complete office, or for just a small computer station? Will an expandable dining table fit?

Because you've just spent a bundle on a security deposit and the first month's rent, **the money left for furnishings may be limited, so start by buying only the essentials.** You can wing it very inexpensively on the finishing touches.

Quick Tip

Before shopping for furniture, lay painter's tape on the floor to represent the size of each piece you want. That will give you a realistic idea of the furniture sizes that fit in a given space. Note the measurements, and take them along when you shop.

Sort the Excess

Before you move, it's hard to know exactly which of your possessions will be useful in the new pad, so the tendency is to take most of them with you. Once you're in and everything you want is in place, are you still neck deep in cartons? If so, it's probably time to start asking yourself the tough questions. Do you really need service for 12 if it's usually just you and a couple of friends with Chinese takeout? **Keep in mind how great a room looks when you have just what you need, organized and displayed to advantage.**

Take some of the cartons you've emptied and start some serious sorting. **Use separate boxes: one for the keepers, another for usable things you could donate or give to family and friends, and one for more valuable items that you can sell online or at a yard sale.** When you come across items—particularly clothing—that you haven't used in a couple of years, it's time for a farewell. Your usable clothing, old cookware, linens, and lamps can make a huge difference in the lives of people in need. **Then bite the bullet and fill a BIG carton for garbage pick-up day.** You can do it! Keep repeating "Less stuff equals more space."

Consignment

One way to make money from items you'd normally give away is by selling them through **consignment shops.** Most will offer you cash or store credit. Call first to see what merchandise they accept and what their terms are. This is **a wonderful way to part with special items,** such as brand-name clothing, furniture, and collectibles.

Consignment shops are also a great place to look for the things you're still missing. **A vintage dresser, with all its charm and detail, could be just the piece you need to round out your room.** It might even cost you less than one you could buy from a large discount store—and it will probably be of better quality and last longer, too.

to have & have not

Freecycling

Another way to get the excess out of your house, and maybe even find something you need, is through "freecycling." At freecycle.org, you can become an online member of your local community, where you can **post things you want to give away and read posts from others.** There's a moderator for every community, and everything is free. You just organize a time and place to pick up or exchange items. Freecycling follows the philosophy of "One man's trash is another man's treasure."

The purpose of this grassroots nonprofit organization is to **save resources and reduce the amount of waste that ends up in landfills.** And it's soothing to know that your beloved, yet cluttering, collection of teacups is going to a good home. Check out the Web site and see whether freecycling is something that interests you.

Donation

Clutter reduces focus and energy, thereby creating stress. **When every item in your house has a place of its own— and a bit of open space around it— you'll find that you feel happier and more productive.** If you donate items you no longer use, you're not only creating a healthier space for yourself, but also making a difference in someone

else's life. So you can feel good about letting go of your things.

Who wants your donations? There are donation boxes all over your town that take clothing and shoes in good condition. Or you can get in touch with any of the organizations listed below to find out what their hours are and whether they make house calls.

Here are some of the organizations to which you can donate, and what they may need:

❖ **Goodwill Industries (goodwill.org):** anything in reasonably good condition

❖ **The Salvation Army (salvationarmy.org):** anything in reasonably good condition

❖ **Habitat for Humanity (habitat.org):** clean clothing, large and small items in working order

❖ **Charitable thrift shops:** dishes, pots, small appliances, clothes, and books. (When you drop things off, take time to look around. You might find just what you've been looking for at a bargain price, and you'll be contributing to the charity that runs the shop.)

❖ **Local shelters:** bed linens, pj's, toiletries, coats, cleaning supplies

❖ **Animal shelters:** towels, blankets, and sheets—even if they're torn or stained—toys, litter boxes, cat condos, carriers

❖ **Houses of worship:** Call to find out what their specific needs are.

❖ **Schools:** school supplies, such as paper, pens, pencils, crayons, markers, tape, and child-safe scissors; children's clothing, outerwear, and shoes; microwave ovens, working office equipment, and items that can be used for school plays

❖ **Local theater groups:** vintage clothes and furniture appropriate for use as props

to have & have not

Make It a Habit

The most important part of downsizing is maintaining a pare-down attitude. **Don't replace what you've discarded.** Consistently remove unused or unusable items so that you don't have to do another big cleanout. A good rule of thumb: for every new item you bring home, get rid of something similar. A better rule is to get rid of two things.

In addition to buying less, you should be buying smarter. **Find products that serve multiple purposes.** For instance, replacing old measuring cups and spoons with all-in-one devices can clear out clutter and save you a surprising amount of drawer space. The important thing is to **make simplification a lifestyle rather than a weekend project.**

to have & have not

Change of Scenery

Are you wondering how you collected so much stuff? Even after you've pared down and donated things, there still doesn't seem to be enough room. You don't want to get rid of anything that has storage capacity, so get creative and see whether some of the pieces can be used another way. Be flexible—forget about what something is called and think about how it can be used.

Furniture can be just as happy in one room as in another. Bookcases can become colorful room dividers, a baker's rack can work as an open pantry, and an armoire can morph into a cool entertainment center or home office. The drawers from an old dresser can become awesome under-the-bed storage units. Simply add casters (wheels), and you're ready to roll. Small bookcases can be laid on their back and used the same way, and the shelves will make dividers for organizing your stored items. So, repurpose whatever you can. It's not only eco-friendly but budget friendly, too.

Keep an Open Mind

Take a fresh look at what you have, and you'll almost certainly discover some furniture that can earn a new job description. Tables, **nightstands,** storage chests, cabinets, two-drawer files, and bookcases of all sizes **are ideal candidates for serving other functions in different parts of your home.** Most of these pieces have drawers, doors, or shelves, so they can hold anything from reading material and clocks to coasters, games, towels, or catalogs. Give them a chance; **if a piece of furniture doesn't fit in one room, try it in another**—even in a hallway or bathroom.

Fresh Perspective

A storage chest that holds extra blankets and pillows **at the foot of a bed can just as easily serve as a sturdy coffee table in the living room.** In the new setting, it might hold bedding for a sofa bed, but could just as well hold CDs, magazines, and games.

Quick Tip

Tuck a fabric-softener sheet or a bar of soap between linens to keep them smelling fresh until the next time you use them. There's nothing as unattractive to guests as musty-smelling pillowcases and sheets.

Make It Work

If you have an extra dresser that doesn't fit in your bedroom, it may look perfectly at home in the kitchen or dining area—and might be even more functional. Its drawers can hold dishtowels, utensils, pots, pans, and even canned goods. If you top it off with a shelving unit, you'll have created a hutch look-alike, perfect for serving pieces, glassware, and cookbooks. You can just as easily **use a couple of shelves on decorative brackets** to achieve a similar look—one that gives you an excellent space for displaying collectibles and other favorite pieces.

Helpful Little Things

As you reconsider some of your furniture's possibilities, you may want to move some pieces around so they can "audition" in other parts of your home. Trying out arrangements in different scenarios can be easy even if the furniture is hefty. You don't have to enlist help from friends, and you don't have to strain your back, either. You can use plastic discs that make it a piece of cake to move heavy pieces all by yourself, even over carpeting. It's easy—just tip, slip, and slide. The little marvels will last forever—or until somebody borrows and forgets to return them! They do have a habit of disappearing. One way to avoid having them going MIA is to leave them under the corners of a large piece of furniture. This will allow you to move the furniture if you need to get access to a cable or telephone hookup, protect the floor, and make them easily accessible the next time you need them.

change of scenery

A Double Life

Two-piece, L-shaped sofas are traditional "sectionals," but the latest versions are "modular." **Because each seating section can be locked to another, they can be arranged in a U or L shape or, sometimes, as one long piece.** The armless units can also be used as individual chairs. If your living room can't accommodate all of the pieces, give one a chance to shine in the bedroom or den.

More Than a Sofa

Some day you may have so much room that a sofa can just be a sofa; meanwhile, you can **achieve a sense of spaciousness** by selecting well-scaled furnishings that are easy to rearrange and can function in more than one way. You may not have a guest room, but when friends and family visit, you'd like a comfortable place for them to sleep. **A futon or convertible sofa provides the perfect solution.** For a five-star host rating, make up their bed using fresh linens, extra pillows, and a soft quilt. (A mint on the pillow is optional.)

Nifty Alternatives

If you have a perfectly fine sofa that doesn't convert to a bed and don't have room for a futon, **consider less space-consuming items, such as a sleeper chair or sleeper ottoman.** If there isn't space for either of those, **you can store an inflatable bed in a closet** in its own duffle bag until you need it.

Quick Tip

Some of the new futon and sleep-chair models have hidden storage, so you get not only an extra sleep space but also a place for its linens.

a double life

Nesting

A three-for is the ultimate space saver. When guests drop in, **a set of stacked tables gives you extra surface space when you need it.** They're easy to stash and easy to move, and they give you a place for snacks. Backgammon, anyone? Just pull out a table to hold your game board, or **use one as a temporary nightstand for an overnight guest.** Some coffee tables come with pullout nesting tables or seating cubes.

Styled Storage

Sometimes thinking outside the box may lead you to think inside the box. Stack them up! **A group of straw, wood, or fabric-covered boxes will add whimsy and give you a little more hidden storage space.**

Trunks and benches are double-duty workhorses. They're so sturdy, you'll probably keep them for years to come and find a way to use them in each new home. Put one in the living room, and it becomes a solid place to set down a midnight snack; put it in the bedroom to hold an extra comforter; **put it in the entryway,** and you can sit on it while you pull on your boots. And if you hang some wall pockets or baskets above it, you'll have a handy place for keys, gloves, and outgoing mail.

Homage to the Ottoman

Ottomans should win an award for versatility. They're another kind of furniture chameleon. They come in all sizes, shapes, and coverings—leather, all kinds of fabric, and wicker. **Ottomans make wonderful coffee tables,** provide additional seating, and can be used in any room. Many ottomans have **generous hideaway space** beneath removable lids; others have lids that flip over to become sturdy serving trays—and yes, you can rest your feet on them. So, three cheers for ottomans!

Quick Tip

Ottomans get lots of love, attention, and abuse. Keep your new sidekick spiffy by treating it with a soil-resistant spray. Try to buy an ottoman with a removable washable cover or one that you can easily spot-treat.

a double life

chapter 2

Portable Pizzazz

When you've moved into a place that you're pretty certain isn't going to be your forever home, the decorating parameters are not the same as with a "permanent" abode, so you have many different things to consider. Although you may want to make changes to create a more comfortable and enjoyable space, you don't want them to be too time consuming and costly. The best way to go is to minimize effort on the "container" and concentrate on the contents. Purchase furnishings that you really like, but buy them wisely so that they can be used in any future setting. Get creative with accessories, and pick ones that "play well with others."

Wall Color...
with and without Paint

Many rental dwellings are freshly painted white or off-white, and often the new occupant is forbidden to paint the walls. That makes some people pretty unhappy; they think white walls are just plain boring. But really, what an opportunity those walls offer! Everything you put within them or on them will look special, which is exactly why some people wouldn't have anything but white walls. Think about how fantastic art galleries look with splashes of color on their white walls. **Even black-and-white artwork and photographs look striking on white walls.** If you have vivid wall hangings, photos, paintings, or sculpture, white may be just right for showing them at their best. **It will brighten and visually expand the size of a room,** and each wall accessory will appear even more remarkable, afloat in its own space.

Art as Inspiration

White walls can set the stage for utter serenity. A plant, mellow art piece, and a variety of subtle textures can transform a room into a romantic dreamscape.

If you're someone who craves color—and your lease permits painting—you may have a good idea of the hues that suit your style. If you're not absolutely sure, visit popular paint manufacturers' Web sites. Most of them have examples of trendy ideas that will inspire you. **Find out whether you are drawn to watery blues or gravitate toward warm earth tones.** Maybe you'll want to be drenched in yellow sunshine or sizzle in fire-engine red.

wall color...with and without paint

Virtually Painted

Before rushing out for painting supplies, here are a few ways to help you make the final choice. Many paint companies offer a selection of color samples in small, inexpensive containers—with just enough paint to cover a square foot of your wall. That way you can **see how the color looks with the things you have, as well as how it looks in changing light at different times of the day.**

Another cool way of previewing the results: you can upload a photo of your room to a few paint manufacturers' sites and get access to a rainbow of colors to try on your own virtual walls. Using this tool allows you to try as many colors (and techniques) as you want, and you'll know exactly what to buy before you shop and invite friends over for a painting party.

Paint Effects

For some areas, you might want to add a little oomph, so consider using some stencil designs, which are a lot more sophisticated than the buttercup and English ivy of years ago. **For drama and depth, and a neat way of hiding minor structural flaws, sponge painting is the way to go.** It's easy and a lot of fun to apply, and you can re-do any section that doesn't make you happy. Another way to add drama and color without a lot of work is to **paint only one wall of a room.**

Quick Tip

Check out the paint department at your home-improvement store. It usually has drastically reduced paints that customers changed their minds about after the colors were mixed. The quantities are generally just right for painting one or two walls.

Cool Hang Ups

What can you do **if your landlord says that painting the walls is absolutely not allowed,** but you still crave color all around you? Easy. You can satisfy that hunger without a single gallon of paint. **Try a fabric fix.** Measure the area you want to cover, and then start hunting for fabric, but not necessarily in a fabric store. You might have better luck finding **sheets or curtains** (in the perfect color, of course) at a discount store or thrift shop. If you have old sheets or curtains of your own, you can use them as they are or take the project up a notch by first tie-dying them or applying fabric paint. You can also **cut the fabric into equal pieces and hang the panels.**

Applying Fabric to a Wall

DECORATING KIT

- ❖ Measuring tape
- ❖ Fabric scissors
- ❖ Nonaerosol spray starch
- ❖ Fabric
- ❖ Pushpins
- ❖ Clean, dry paint roller

1. Take the measurements of the area that you intend to cover.

2. Cut the fabric to size, allowing an extra 2 in. for trimming the top and bottom.

3. Spray the top half of the wall with a nonaerosol liquid starch.

4. Place the fabric over the starched area, and temporarily secure it at the top with pushpins.

5. Go over the fabric surface with a clean, dry paint roller, smoothing out any creases.

6. Spray the remaining half of the wall with the starch, and apply the fabric in the same way until the wall is covered.

7. Inspect the surface. If there are any remaining wrinkles, spray them lightly with the starch and work them out with the roller.

8. Trim excess fabric, and remove the pushpins.

Colorful Curtains

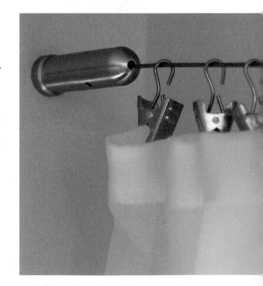

Curtains are not just for windows anymore. **Rod systems can be mounted high on windowless walls** or from the ceiling. And by hanging flat panels of fabric from them, **you'll add wide swaths of color to your space.** Because some rods can go around corners, the hanging fabric can provide privacy for a study area or hide a little mess (such as the stack of boxes you haven't unpacked yet). **Tension rods are an especially handy and damage-free solution for hanging fabrics.**

Indoor Scenery

Wall murals are a stylish color option. **A wall can be transformed into a tropical beach,** a Manhattan skyline, or a Paris café. The murals can be camp, sophisticated, or **serene scenes to match your mood.** The downside is that they tend to dominate the space, so you need to select a scene that you won't tire of quickly. Most wall murals can be put up using removable adhesive and come off without difficulty. There are also fabric murals printed on semi-sheer panels that you can hang from a rod placed at ceiling height.

Good Graffiti

For adding a lot of personality, there's a wide range of vinyl wall decals that simply cling without glue of any kind. Does your space lack architectural detail? **Use decals to mimic chair rail, molding, and wainscoting.** Abstract and floral designs liven up blank walls, and word and letter decals are charming eye-catchers. They're witty and fun, and they say something about who you are.

Don't stop there: **you can use wall decals on almost any smooth surface.** Place a graphic on posterboard and frame it for instant art. Spice up your storage bins, shower curtain, trash cans, or dresser drawers. You can use the decals on windows for added privacy, too. Some places even have decals made to fit your laptop computer!

The number of removable wall-graphic retailers out there is astounding. At least one of them is bound to have something you like. (Look for information on a few of these retailers in "Resources," on page 160.)

The New Tapestry

Does the word "tapestry" make you think of old castles and big price tags? If so, you're in for a pleasant surprise. **Contemporary tapestries** feature awesome designs in rich colors. If you're aiming for a Southwestern look, hang a Native American-inspired blanket or rug on the wall and then add some earth tones and clay accessories, and you're almost there. All you need now are a few cactus plants. If you're leaning toward French country, try hanging a few yards of printed toile. And for an ethnic style, consider batik and Kente cloth, which **can be as bold and as beautiful as paintings.** Add a few masks or a tall vase (or an umbrella stand) of dried branches for more character. Whichever style you're creating, just **look for patterns and colors that will add spice to the overall flavor of the room.**

Art in 3-D

When you're mounting objects on the wall, you'll get a lot more zing if they relate to a single theme. Metal sculpture, masks, and **wood carvings make beautiful visual music** alone or in a grouping. And speaking of music, if you play an instrument, you might try hanging it on the wall (as long as it's not a bassoon or cello). Instruments are gorgeous on view. Also, the wall is a safe place to keep them until you're ready to jam.

cool hang ups

Picture This

A single large piece of artwork can set the tone for your entire space. So if you already own a special painting, give it the star treatment and **pick up its colors and patterns as you decorate around it.** If you don't have a painting that really turns you on, treasure hunting for one is a treat all by itself. Artwork doesn't have to be a budget buster. You might find just what you're looking for at a live or online auction, at an art show, in a discount store, in a craft or thrift shop, or even at a yard sale.

You can also create your own wall art in so many ways and so inexpensively. You'll have such a great time doing it that you'll look for reasons to create more. One way is to cut a large, colorful poster into even sections; put each part in an identical frame; and hang them in a group. Or buy a few rolls of fabulous gift wrap in different patterns but in the same colors, and then **hit the local hobby shop for mats and frames.** Another method is to take two to four sections of patterned fabric and frame them—or neatly wrap them around matching plywood rectangles, and staple them to the back.

Art Arrangements

Want to have some **awesome artwork that picks up the major colors** in your room? Remember those little spin-art sets for kids? Try this amazing trick: buy or borrow one; choose the colors you want; and spin out a "masterpiece." Any office supply store will enlarge it for you, and then you can frame it with a lightweight poster frame. It will look like a pricey print from an art gallery or museum shop.

Try to remember that **grouping small and medium-size pictures is like planting flower bulbs—odd numbers often work best.** A variety of shapes will also add excitement. Artwork is most effective at eye level, but that's not a rule written in stone. So experiment with placement, and discover what works best for you.

Quick Tip

Explore fabric paints; they can add texture and dimension where you need it most. Before you frame that piece of fabric, highlight parts of it using paint to match the fabric. Metallic paints are perfect for adding some oomph to a dull picture.

Art Groupies

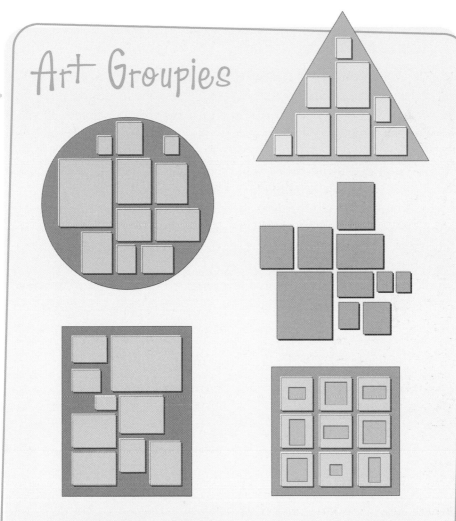

If you want to hang multiple pictures without the trial-and-error routine that leaves lots of holes, try this:

1. Cut newspaper or brown wrapping paper to the same sizes as all the pictures you want to hang.

2. Tape the paper to the wall using painter's blue masking tape. The tape lets you rearrange the papers to your heart's content.

3. Once you have them just the way you want the pictures to hang, replace each piece of paper with the real thing. The tape will come right off without leaving a mark.

A New Frame of Mind

Years ago, photography was primarily thought of as a tool for capturing family memories or recording historical events. But for some time now, photography has been fully recognized as an art form—and a pretty fabulous one. **For flat-out drama, there's nothing like black and white photos.** And you can even take them yourself. Have your favorite images enlarged, and then showcase them effectively in simple mats and frames. **Mix similarly themed paintings and pictures for a chic gallery look.**

A few words about frames: thrift shops and yard sales are ideal places to pick up bargain frames. You can always discard the "art" that comes with it if the frame is a size and shape you like. Then all it might need is a coat of paint to become a perfect accessory.

If the framed artwork you're installing is lightweight, **try one of the new**

Picture this

easel hooks, suction, or removable adhesive methods. In any case, hanging pictures using traditional methods can be done with little or no damage to the walls. Professional brass-plated hooks have super skinny nails that are easy to remove, and the holes can be repaired in seconds. (See "How to Fix Small Holes," page 147.) **The space between two of the "teeth" would fit neatly over a removable hook, also.** Even the old standard picture-hanging hardware doesn't call for anchors, so when you remove it, you won't be taking out chunks of the wall. But if you're hanging something heavy, you may need to secure it using anchors.

If you have a frame that doesn't have a hanging wire and is too hard for cyc-pins that hold wire, look for a small saw-tooth metal strip that's usually with other picture hanging paraphernalia in home-improvement stores. This hook is held in place by the edge of the frame rather than by pins. Position it at the exact center at the top of the back of the frame.

Screen Scene

Owning a folding screen is **like having a spare wall** you can stand up wherever you need it. Want a partition to separate your study/desk area from the rest of the dining room? Want to hide a door to the utility closet? How about giving a guest bed some privacy? **Maybe you just want to add color or texture to the room.** Whatever its use, whatever kind of furnishings you have, there's bound to be a screen that will do the job. You'll find well-priced varieties in wood and fabric. Even an opaque fireplace screen can be put to work around the house to hide a litter box or a couple of recycling bins.

Fabric Screens

An imaginative way to look at the screen idea is to hang fabric from the ceiling to divide a space. For a permanent divider, you can simply hang a bed sheet from the ceiling. **If you want a somewhat translucent divider—for instance, if there is only one window providing light for one large space—use a sheer, white sheet.** For an opaque divider, and some added color, use a sheet that complements your decor. As long as what you use to mount the sheet is sturdy, you can even hang two different-color sheets together so that both sides work with their respective decor. **Another neat idea is to mount a very large shade between rooms.** This way, you can lower the shade when you want privacy, or raise the shade when you want one large, cohesive look in the space.

How to Build a Three-Panel Folding Screen

You can make your own folding screen easily and for very little money, too. Use lightweight (hollow) flat-panel doors that are not too wide (closet-size), louver doors, or shutters. You can find all of the above at any home-improvement store, but if there's a building salvage company in your area, you might want to check it out first. You never know what treasures you might find—perhaps a few wonderful old doors or shutters. A vintage door divided into three panels could be a handsome alternative, but make sure it isn't covered in lead-based paint. Even plywood cut to the desired size will do the job, and you can decorate it any number of ways.

DECORATING KIT

- Measuring tape
- Pencil
- 6 standard or double-action (optional) hinges
- Screws
- Drill
- Screwdriver
- 3 door panels

1. Measure and mark the sides of the panels at three equidistant points from the top to the bottom—generally, a quarter of the way down from the top and up from the bottom, and the midpoint between the two.

2. Lay the panels on a large flat surface. Line up the top of each hinge with a mark, and predrill the holes.

3. Line up the hinges, and screw them into place.

4. If you are not using double-action hinges, which allow the screen to fold in either direction, reverse the hinges on the last panel.

Screens Aplenty

There are (almost) infinite ways to customize DIY folding screens. Here are just a few ideas to inspire your artistry:

* Paint both sides of each door with a color that picks up a major hue in the room. After the first coat is dry, apply a second color lightly with a sponge.
* Paint all sides of each door the same color as your sofa or walls. Buy a smaller quantity of an accent color (one that picks up the colors of your throw pillows, rug, or lamps). After the first

coat of paint is thoroughly dry, use a stencil to apply your accent color. (A small design may get lost on a large surface, so try a bold one.)

❖ Paint only the edges of the doors; then cover the fronts (and backs, if you wish) with wallpaper. Prepasted vinyl is the easiest wallpaper to apply.

❖ Decorate with die-cut wallpaper borders, which are even more interesting when they are applied vertically.

❖ Apply wallpaper to part or all of each door. Be sure to measure carefully and cut the wallpaper to the exact size. (Using a T-square will help to keep your lines straight.) Don't forget to smooth out any bubbles in the paper.

❖ Apply fabric to part or all of each door. (If you'd like to change up the look, see "How to Apply Fabric to a Wall," page 39.)

❖ Decoupage each door. Glue old photos, clippings, postcards, or any other paper item that's special to you on the doors. You can also decoupage with fabric. The medium is sold in all crafts stores and comes with simple directions. Be sure to finish your project using a clear, nonyellowing top coat.

❖ Decorate alternate sides differently for a reversible look. If the screen will be a room divider, coordinate each side with the room it's facing.

If you're using old shutters, you'll need to clean and paint them before attaching them to each other. Again, if the shutters are vintage, they may have lead paint, in which case you should forgo painting them and leave them shabby but chic. If you're using new shutters, painting is also optional. And if you're going to hang objects on them, turn them upside down—that is, with the larger opening of each slat facing upward. That will allow you to insert a hook more easily. Once you insert a few hooks, you can hang objects from them, such as strands of beads, greeting card keepers, scarves, or plants.

Floors to Go

Maybe you've lucked out and your new place has gleaming wood floors or a brand new carpet, but it's more likely that the first thing that comes to mind when you look down is "How can I hide this?" The great news is that not only can you cover ugly floors with attractive new materials, but you may be able to take the new cover-ups with you the next time you move. **Laminates are an ideal solution for living rooms, bedrooms, halls, and dining areas, and even kitchens and baths.** Resilient vinyl is another affordable option that's perfect for bathrooms and kitchens.

Looks Like the Real Thing

Laminate flooring has a lot going for it. For starters, it comes in boxes that can be carried and that easily fit in a car. Installation is simple—you can install it over an existing floor. It's a one- or two-person job that doesn't involve nails, glue, or odor, and you can walk on the floor immediately. **Laminates can mimic wood, tile, and other natural materials.** Another wonderful thing about laminates is that you can **put them down over linoleum, vinyl, ceramic tile, or any other flat surface.** Some kinds can be removed easily, too. So down the road, if you love your laminate floors, you may be able to reuse them in your next home.

Installing a Laminate Floor

The manufacturers provide installation directions, and it's important to read and follow their guidelines. If you don't, you may invalidate the warranty. Here are a few things to help you get started:

DECORATING KIT

- ❧ Laminate flooring spacers
- ❧ Foam underlayment padding
- ❧ Installation block
- ❧ Circular saw or handsaw
- ❧ Chalk line
- ❧ Soft wood block
- ❧ Pencil

- ❧ Prepare the room for the project by thoroughly cleaning the floor.
- ❧ Once you bring the laminate planks home, remove them from the packaging and let them acclimate to the room environment for 48 hours.
- ❧ Lay some loose boards across the room, and decide which way you want them to go. Do they look better set down across the length or across the width of the room? You may prefer laying the planks diagonally in order to give the room an illusion of greater space.

1. Make sure the existing flooring is in sound condition; then roll out the foam padding starting at one corner. If you are covering a concrete slab, most manufacturers require you to lay a polyethylene vapor barrier underneath the foam.

2. Lay boards from left to right, starting in the left corner of the room. Connect the first row of boards by gently tapping the ends together to ensure a tight joint. Install plastic spacers wherever the boards meet a wall. The gaps created by these spacers give the floor room to expand and contract.

3. If you can't push a board in place using only your hands, then gently drive the boards together using the grooved installation block. Don't strike the block too hard because this might cause damage to the tongue on the board.

4. To measure the perimeter boards that need cutting, first lay a full plank over the last installed board. Push a third board against the wall, and run a pencil along its edge to mark the cutting line. Make the cut using a circular saw and a fine-tooth blade.

Easy as...

1... 2... 3.

Carpeting Piece by Piece

If you just need to cover the existing carpet in a small, worn, or stained area, consider using an area rug. Some have unusual shapes that will do the job. If you want to cover every inch of a carpet that you really dislike and can't remove, check out the latest in **large carpet squares.** They have a clever interlocking system, so the pieces can be attached to each other and not to the floor surface. **Carpet tiles** come in a variety of colors and textures and **can be configured to fit any space or size.** They stay in place and behave like a brand-new carpet, but **can be picked up in a flash to be used again and again, or replaced when damaged.**

If the floor in your kitchen only inspires you to eat out, **consider using a similar interlocking system made of vinyl.** It comes in manageable sections that are look-alikes of wooden plank flooring, slate, and stone, and they're **exceptionally durable and easy to clean.** They also work wonders in bathrooms that need a fresh look.

floors to go

Built-In Bluffs

Modular wall units are especially smart purchases for temporary quarters. Their design has so much flexibility that it's a sure bet **you'll be able to reuse them in different ways and in different spaces.**

The trick to making modular units look like one large built-in is to fill an entire wall with them, even arranging them around windows and doors. If you think that would look overbearing, select units that match, or come close to matching, your wall color. For just a splash of color, paint just the inside, behind the shelves.

You can also get a built-in look in the corner of a room by butting two bookcases against one another at the corner and topping them off with trim that disguises the space between them.

How good can it get? **A wall of varied modular sections has shelves** to display many of your favorite things, **cabinets** for easy access to less-aesthetic necessities, **drawers, and room for storage baskets**—and it looks so uncluttered that people who don't know you better might think you're compulsively neat.

Style Sense

When people walk through your door for the first time, what they see is a bit of your autobiography. They'll get a "read" on what your interests are, clues to your personality, and a sense of what's important to you. Think of all the things your home might say: comfort is a priority; isn't afraid of color; seems pretty organized; et cetera. A peek into the kitchen is a giveaway, too: maybe there's a bulletin board with a dozen take-out menus, or a spice rack with half-empty jars. Is the seating in the living room arranged for conversation or for watching movies? Are the vibes sentimental, whimsical, serene, or adventurous? As you put together the things that make up your unique style, you may even get to know yourself better!

Focus on Favorites

Is there a decorating style that has your name written on it? Do you even need to have a specific favorite? Not when there are so many attractive ways to mix and match. **What's most important is that your home pleases you** and that you're visually and literally comfortable in it.

If you're not quite sure what style you want, just **think of all the rooms you've ever visited or seen that made you feel most at home.** Aim for that look, and tweak it until it suits you perfectly. Whether the style you want is shabby chic, ethnic, contemporary, country, or retro flea-market, you can do it. Meanwhile, just call what you have "eclectic"— you never know, **eclectic may turn out to be the perfect fit.**

Find a Focal Point

At one time or another, most people find themselves with a collection of mismatched furnishings, but your goal can still be reached, and the journey will be more enjoyable than you could have imagined. You just need a point of view, so **start with a focus piece—something that you really love.** Although a painting may be the first thing that comes to mind, **it could be anything that has meaning for you: an old bentwood rocking chair, a tray of river stones, or a beautiful sculpture**—anything. Then give it the royal treatment by keeping its pattern, texture, and color scheme in mind as you shop for additional furnishings.

Hide & Seek

If you want light to come through your windows but hate the view, **try using paper shades.** They start at under $10 and can be installed without nails, drills, screws, or brackets.

Staying with the light-but-not-the-sight goal, stop in at your local home improvement store to see the **vinyl films** that you can cut to size and apply to your windows using a squeegee. They're available in a variety of finishes and designs—frosted, stained glass, wrought iron, floral, and abstract—and they **can be peeled off easily.**

How to Frost a Window

1. Clean the glass, and let it dry completely.

2. Mask the area around the glass, such as the window sash, the sill, and the casing. You can use plain brown paper or newspaper.

3. Make sure the room is ventilated. (It's a good idea to wear gloves and a respirator, too.)

4. Working side to side, apply a single thin coat of paint, slightly overlapping each consecutive pass. Let the finish stand for 30 minutes in order to dry completely.

5. Once the paint is thoroughly dry, apply a second coat in the same manner.

Window Solutions

Many styles of **woven blinds and fabric honeycomb shades can be mounted to open from both the top and bottom.** In addition to being able to adjust incoming light at different times of day, you'll also have the opportunity to **view a lot more sky and much less parking lot.**

For times when you want to see out your window but don't want the favor completely returned, café curtains may be a sweet retro solution.

Using sheer curtains on **tension rods** is a nice, **easy way of eliminating glare while still getting light, privacy, and atmosphere.**

Years ago, the choice of tension rod styles was minimal, but now there are a number of finishes and shapes, and happily, no hardware or tools are required—not even for longer, 84- or 96-inch lengths.

Quick Tip

For fast and easy no-sew curtains, slide a tension rod inside a sheet's wide hem. Even better, use sheets that complement your bed linen for a custom look.

hide & seek

Tie-back Tricks

If your view is to-die-for (and you're game for making a few holes), call attention to it with tieback curtains or panels. Then go for some **low-cost, high-style panache** by passing on elaborate metal tieback hardware and using decorative scarves and ribbons instead.

Try something whimsical, such as those bendable faux flowers you find at craft stores. For a masculine touch, use a couple of men's ties. And for high marks in repurposing, hold those curtains aside with hair accessories, such as bands and clips.

Get Cushy

Often, the **soft touches** make a room feel exceptionally welcoming. If a down-filled easy chair isn't in your budget, you can still get a warm and cozy feeling with a little improvisation. **Add things that feel good to the touch:** squishy pillows covered in velvet, suede, or faux fur; a chenille or fleece throw; or **an area rug that makes your bare feet happy.**

Soften in Small Doses...

Because so many of the large pieces of furniture have hard finishes, using soft and stylish fabric accents gives rooms a tactile balance. **A gorgeous tablecloth can make meat loaf seem like beef Wellington** (almost, anyway). Table scarves and runners have recently made a comeback, too. At one time, you only saw them on special occasions, but now they're adding charm on a daily basis. **Many runners are reversible, so don't worry about little mishaps;** just flip them over. (No one has to know.) That's also one less item that needs to be stored! The fabric's soft texture complements the table's solidity and **provides a splash of color** that sets the stage for your dishes and candles. Dress up the table, and every meal will look festive.

get cushy

...Or in Big Ways

The bedroom spotlights soft goods on the largest piece of furniture in the room, so **put a little zing in your "Zs."** Whether the bed is a huge California king, a queen-size, a standard twin, or a folding cot, **lovely bed linens can add style as well as comfort.**

If you just have a mattress and box spring on a basic metal frame, there are a few ways to **make your bed look special.** You could **add some shelves above it for accessories and lighting,** display a focal-point painting, or use posh linens. You can also hang color-coordinated fabric behind the bed to give everything a finished look.

Quick Tip

When choosing new bed linens, look at the thread count. The higher the count, the softer and silkier the sheets feel. And quality linens feel more luxurious with age.

How to Make an Upholstered Headboard

If you're determined to have a headboard, consider making an upholstered one yourself. It's budget friendly, nice and cushy, and fairly simple to construct. Best of all, you'll be able to pat yourself on the back for the effort every morning and every night. To make the job even easier, choose a fabric that stretches a little.

DECORATING KIT

- Fabric, cut to size, allowing an extra 4 in. all around
- Plywood cut to size (or an old wooden headboard)
- Two 30-in. 2x4s to use as "legs"
- 2- to 3-in.-thick foam, cut to size, allowing an extra 2 in. all around
- Upholstery batting, cut to size, allowing an extra 3 in. all around
- Staple gun ❖ Drill ❖ Screws ❖ Screwdriver

1. Determine the size of the board. Typically, a double bed is 54 in. wide and a queen-size model is 60 in. To be sure, measure the width of the mattress. You'll want the headboard to extend beyond the mattress by a couple of inches on each side. You can make it as tall as you like. To get the height, start by measuring up from the point between the mattress and box spring. You'll probably want it to be at least 3 to 4 ft. high.

2. Pull the foam over all four sides of the plywood, and staple it to the back of the board.

3. Do the same thing with the batting, allowing an additional 3 in. all around the board.

4. Iron the fabric, and then lay it face down on a clean, flat surface.

5. Place the board on the fabric with the foam and batting face down. Start stapling at the top in the center, and pull the fabric just tightly enough so that the front is smooth. Put a few staples at the bottom, and continue along the sides, checking frequently to make sure the front remains tight and doesn't pucker.

6. Attach the "legs." But first measure them again to make sure they'll bring the headboard to the height you want. Use screws to fasten the legs to either side of the headboard, about 3 in. from each edge.

Some metal bed frames have premade holes to accommodate headboard attachments, but if yours doesn't, you can attach the headboard legs directly to the wall. Or simply lean the headboard against the wall; the mattress and box spring will hold it in place.

Light It Up

There are times that dim light is truly romantic, but that's not what you want when you're slicing veggies, putting on makeup, or trying to read. **It's essential that you have plenty of light where and when you need it.** Ample light is not only good for your eyes, it does wonders for your spirit, so grab it where you can! **The easiest, most eco-friendly way to double the daytime infusion of sunlight through your windows is to simply use a few well-placed mirrors.**

Supplement the Basics

If the overhead light fixtures in your temporary dwelling don't do the job, there's no reason to be left in the dark. The solutions are plentiful. Stand-alone floor lamps can provide extra lighting, and many of them come with several "arms" that you can aim wherever you like.
Clip on, desk, pendant, and table lamps are excellent choices for brightening specific areas.

light it up

Creative Lighting

Too often, the selection of **tabletop lamps** is taken lightly. In addition to their obvious function, they **can really add some glamour to a room.**

You shouldn't skimp on light, but you can cut the cost of the fixtures. It doesn't matter whether a lamp comes from a yard sale, a thrift shop, or a lucky dumpster dive. If it is in working order, is sturdy, and has a shape and size you like, it's a "find." Take it home; **it can always be painted or covered, and topped off with a new shade.** Keep in mind that wrought iron, brass, and copper lamp bases take paint well and are especially forgiving of careless handling (children, pets, and moving).

Quick Tip

How about creating a little aroma therapy? Add a few drops of your favorite fragrance to a scent ring that is placed on top of a light bulb and releases the scent into the air.

Functional Lighting

You may not do a lot of cooking, but you still don't want to accidentally open a can of beans when you thought you grabbed the tomato soup. **Light is an absolute must in the kitchen.** Unfortunately, an overhead fixture usually doesn't cut it. There's no need to fumble anymore. **Illuminate cabinets and countertops (or for that matter, artwork and bookcases) inexpensively using stick-on, long-lasting LED lights.**

Some compact lights go beyond the basic on/off switch and have sensors that respond to hand movement. Pass your hand near it once, and it provides dim, almost romantic light; pass by it again, and the light gets bright; one more time and the light goes off. Some even have a built-in, automatic one-hour shutoff feature. This gem of a light fixture can **brighten a bathroom or closet** equally well.

light it up

Light Where You Need It

If the night table in your bedroom holds a clock radio, a couple of books, and a phone, you might want to consider another place for a lamp. If you have an overhead shelf or headboard, **you'll be able to finish your "who-done-it" with the help of a neat slide-on or clip-on lamp** or a couple of wall-mounted light fixtures.

Quick Tip

For mood lighting without matches, try a few flameless candles. The better models are battery-operated and even simulate the flickering of a real flame.

Movable Ambiance

Perhaps the most welcoming item in a living room is a fireplace, and now anyone who has a few feet of wall space can have one. **The electric and gel-flame units have all the ambiance and none of the work of masonry-and-flue fireplaces.** No yearly expense for a professional chimney-sweep service, and no hauling logs or scooping ashes. Best of all, this kind of fireplace is completely portable. It can move as easily as any other piece of furniture, so don't dream of leaving it behind. If there's not enough wall space for it in the living room, let it **add some romance to the bedroom or dining area.**

How about a flameless fireplace? With a little bit of luck, **you can get an authentic fireplace look with an old mantel from a construction salvage yard.** Set it against a wall; put a few pictures or candles on the ledge; and set a couple of plants at the bottom. Voila! You have a fireplace that looks as if it came with the room.

Neat Stuff

You have better things to do with your time than hunt for a receipt, the electric bill, or a phone number you scribbled on the back of an envelope. "Homeless" items can cause headaches as well as clutter. **Once your belongings all have a designated place, you'll discover space you didn't know you had** and gain a few extra hours each week for something more enjoyable than plowing through piles of loose papers. So let's start with those papers.

If you don't have a file cabinet, you can use an accordion file for paid bills and receipts and **a pocket folder or wall pocket for bills coming due.** You can drastically cut down on the amount of paper—and save a few trees while you're at it—by **receiving and paying bills online.** You still may want to print out the payment confirmations, but at least you've saved several sheets of paper, envelopes, and postage. Above all, you've lowered your carbon footprint and saved space.

Trim the Fat in Your Files

Wondering how long you need to keep papers? That depends on what they are:

❖ Paycheck stubs: 1 year (When you receive your W-2 form, make sure the info on your stubs matches. If it does, you can toss the stubs.)
❖ Paid bills: 1 year (Toss them after you have the cancelled checks.)
❖ Bank register, statements, deposit slips, cancelled checks: 7 years
❖ Tax returns and supporting documentation: 7 years
❖ Insurance records: life of policy, plus 10 years
❖ Contracts and leases: full term of contract, plus 3 years
❖ Car title: duration of ownership
❖ Lease: until you get your security deposit back!

Papers to keep FOREVER:
❖ Birth certificates
❖ Death certificates
❖ Marriage and divorce certificates
❖ Wills
❖ Social security cards
❖ Citizenship documents
❖ Military records
❖ Special awards
❖ Diplomas
❖ Transcripts
❖ Medical history
❖ IRA contributions
❖ Oh, and of course, love letters.

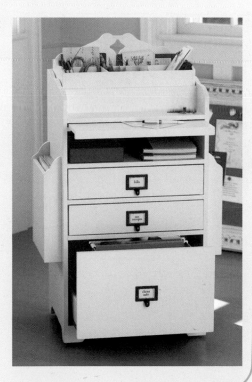

Everyone Needs a Bookcase

With the exception of a fireplace, nothing says home quite as warmly, or as efficiently, as a group of bookcases. In addition to giving those accordion folders a home of their own, **you can store your must-keep periodicals in magazine holders, and set them on a shelf.** Display some photos, sculpture, shells, sets of handsome storage boxes, and your favorite board games, and you'll still have room for many books. Besides their storage capacity, structural interest, and color, bookcases have an inherent appeal—**they look terrific wherever you put them.**

Vertical Storage

When space is limited, **the back of a closet door needs to do more than provide a hook for your bathrobe.** And there are dozens of organizing products that will turn that nearly forgotten space into a big-time storage solution. With no nails and no fuss, they rest securely on the top of the door. These versatile space savers are enormously varied. **Some designs are perfect for holding shoes—as many as 36 pairs.** Others hold piles of folded tees and sweaters in the bedroom or towels for the bathroom. And still others include clips to hold purses, hats, and other accessories.

Utilize All Available Space

What about **the inside of your closet?** It's probably safe to assume it's not a 10- x 12-foot walk-in with a window and maple built-ins. Still, you can make even a small closet work overtime. Start by looking up. **There's usually enough height for at least a couple of shelves,** and by stacking storage containers of the same size, you can neatly store out-of-season clothing and free up hanger space.

No matter what size your closet is, using reasonably priced closet organizers—which have shelves, pullout bins, racks, drawers, and inserts—will help you **customize the space to suit yourself** and can be reconfigured in future digs.

Double Up

For even more room, **install a double-rod system.** You could use a strong adjustable tension rod if you're only going to hang lightweight items. (A tension rod won't hold up to the same stress as a properly installed closet rod.) They're easy to find, and spring into action without any help from nails, screws, or brackets. And someday, when it's no longer needed in your closet, it can be used as a curtain or shower rod, or for a partition; **tension rods also make excellent temporary clothes-drying racks.**

Slim Down

If your shoes are already stored in a door rack, you'll have plenty of room for a second closet rod and any additional hanging organizers. While wire hangers take up little space, they ruin the shape of your clothes. But the **"good" hangers are often bulky and take up too much room on the rod.** To gain even more space, you can purchase smartly designed ultra-thin, nonslip hangers, and multipiece hangers. **For items you won't need for months, use vacuum-seal bags in which you can compress the clothing using your household vacuum cleaner.** Another solution is to use hanger organizers, which allow up to five or six items to hang vertically rather than horizontally. Some of these are one-piece plastic or metal strips, while others attach one-piece-to-a-hanger to hold the next hanger down from it. It's amazing the way cool organizing items can practically double your closet space.

neat stuff

Wardrobes

No closet in your bedroom? Once in a while that happens. But cheer up; you don't have to live out of storage containers and cardboard boxes. You have great choices. **There are many freestanding wardrobes in stylish finishes that you'll be able to take with you and use again and again.** If you have a closet in the new place, just install a few more shelves and **you can use the wardrobe in the living room as an entertainment center,** in the kitchen as a pantry, or in the dining room as a hutch. There are also wheel-around fabric wardrobes that look like oversize garment bags. You can easily collapse and disassemble them when you're ready to move.

Quick Tip

Many handsome wooden wardrobes come with removable shelves and rods so that, in the future, they can be converted to media centers or hideaway offices.

Chapter 3 Style Sense

Display Your Utensils

Kitchen storage is easier than you might think. You know you can keep dishes, glassware, utensils, and food in cupboards, drawers, and cabinets, but what about all the rest of the stuff? The pans, the pots, their lids? How about the colander, the steamer, the whisks, and slotted spoons? Don't let them drive you up the wall—put them *on* the wall. **The wall is bonus space for all kinds of hooks, magnetic strips for knives and spice holders, sleek stainless-steel rods, and racks for the hard-to-store items.**

The walls can also host wooden or stainless-steel shelves that will give you places for canisters, mixing bowls, serving pieces, and cookbooks. When you get right down to it, the kitchen is probably the only room where things can be left hanging out. Instead of looking like clutter, they can be decorative, functional, and at hand when you need them.

neat stuff

chapter 4

Dorms & Small Digs

Small spaces don't have to cramp your style; they don't even have to look small. Once you learn how to maximize the potential of an item or a room, you'll find that you have plenty of extra space. All it takes is a little bit of practical magic—and some pretty inventive pieces of furniture. Decorating tricks conceal unsightly storage, and simple organizational solutions create a place for everything. Explore cool ways to turn a tiny kitchen into a fully functional space; find out how high-traffic bathrooms can be clutter free; create a comfortable bedroom that serves multiple purposes; and conjure a home office or closet from thin air.

Airspace

Whether it's in a dorm, a one-room studio, or shared quarters, **the key to living comfortably and harmoniously is realistic planning** and organization. When you're told to utilize every available inch, it doesn't mean fill every inch. It just means store things in ways that don't gobble up precious floor space. In tight quarters, recognizing and using vertical space is the key. Clearly, **hanging things from the walls and ceilings can account for a lot of the space you'll gain, but when items must be set on the floor, try to find ones that maximize vertical space.** (Think of what builders do when space is at a premium: they build up.) The point is that there's extra square footage hiding in every room and every hallway. It just takes a little imagination to use the space.

The New Junk Drawer

Whether you're coming or going, hats and gloves, coats, umbrellas, **keys, cell phones, and chargers should be near the front door.** You don't need a foyer—just a little bit of wall space, and you can **hang an all-in-one unit to do the job.** Some units come with clocks, mirrors, key hooks, and cubbies for mail.

Small Spaces Work Hard

If you have a hallway that's wide enough for a **bench or console table with storage,** you're already maximizing usable space. But don't forget to look up, as well. Attach a neat shelf unit or simply make your own using 1x4s and decorative brackets. If you keep the shelves at shoulder height, whatever you put on them is safe from being accidentally knocked over as you carry in groceries. **A hallway is also a handy place for a corkboard message center because it's hard not to see a message as you come in the door.**

Hang Around

New plasma and LCD TVs have thin screens that can hang on a wall, but even if you're still enjoying a bulky model, **you can free up floor space by using a wall-mounted shelf for that old TV.** When you upgrade your TV, you can repurpose the shelf for your surround sound system. Eventually, when moving time comes around again, you'll have to take out all of the hardware, and fill the holes with spackling compound.

There are plenty of inventive ways to **maximize vertical space,** such as **hanging chairs, hammocks, lights, shelving, and room dividers,** all of which will not only clear the floor but make it a cinch to vacuum.

airspace

From Bookcase to Closet

Closets and armoires are usually a great use of vertical space, especially compared with low dressers that eat up floor space. From the floor up, every inch of space is useful, starting with shoe storage, then maybe some drawers or shelves, a rod for hanging clothes, and finally a couple more shelves for storing less-used items.

If you aren't lucky enough to have a built-in closet, and you don't want to take up space with a second bulky dresser or spend lots of money on a fancy armoire, **you can easily and inexpensively make your own closet using a bookcase.**

airspace

Create a Clothes Closet

DECORATING KIT

- A bookcase or cabinet that is at least 18 in. deep (with adjustable shelves)
- Wooden clothes rod
- Pair of rod sockets with screws
- An opaque readymade curtain or fabric shade
- Tension rod (for a curtain), or
- Mounting hardware (for a shade)
- Measuring tape ❖ Pencil
- Drill ❖ Cleat ❖ Screwdriver

1. Remove the shelves of the bookcase.

2. To determine the width of the rod, measure the inside width of the bookcase and subtract ½ in.

3. To determine the approximate size of the readymade curtain or shade you'll need, measure the outside length and width of the bookcase.

4. Determine how much hanging room you need, lengthwise, in order to know how high or low to install the rod. (Measure the clothes you plan to hang.)

5. Once you determine about how high or low you need the rod to be, install the first rod socket on a side wall about halfway from the back wall. Make small pilot holes for the screws.

6. Install the second rod socket on the opposite wall. Make sure both are even, using a level, before tightening the screws.

7. Create a shoe rack, if you like, by reinstalling one or two shelves near the bottom.

8. If you're using a curtain cover, mount it using a tension rod that can be stretched across the interior walls of the unit. For a shade, install the hardware on the inside of the bookcase at the top. Attach a cleat for the cord to the front of the unit.

Bathroom Strategy

Even a nice-size bathroom seems to shrink to dollhouse proportions when you're sharing it. **Tall, thin cabinets**—especially over-the-toilet units—**with doors and adjustable shelves are a good start toward a harmonious morning.** Each roommate can have a personal shelf, and there should even be some space left over for an extra roll or two of toilet tissue. It's also helpful for each person to have a separate caddie for personal toiletries.

Mounted Storage

A wall-mounted medicine cabinet can hold extra shampoos, moisturizers, and dental supplies. Extra-deep ones can even accommodate bulky items, such as rolls of toilet tissue.

A way to keep magazines off the floor is with a wall-mounted rack. If you want to forgo hardware and holes, there are racks that hang from the side of the toilet tank. Browse through the innovative bathroom accessories available, and you'll be sure to find some that will suit your space.

Quick Tip

A simple way to add some character to your bathroom is by replacing the hardware. You can switch it back when you move out. You can even replace the towel bars with inventive alternatives.

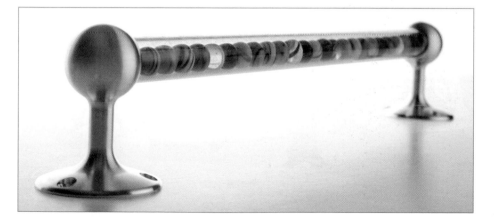

Storage Cubbies: Reinvented

From just one small hook, you can suspend a multitiered basket that provides an extra 72 inches of organized storage. In addition to over-the-door multihook space-savers, there are some with multiple towel rods. No linen closet? No problem. Simply hang a sweater cubby organizer on the outside of the shower rod; it can store your clean towels just where you need them.

bathroom strategy

Sweet Dreams

Besides your comfort, **what things should you think about when choosing a bed?** Of course you'll consider size and price, but it might also be a good idea to **figure out how you'll get it home, if your selection will make it up and through the hallway, and which wall it will fit on.** (A split box spring is the answer when hallways and stairwells are tight squeezes.) Making a good choice is easier when you're familiar with the options, so here are standard bed sizes to help you when you shop:

Twin/Single	39" x 75"
Long Twin*	39" x 80"
Full/Double	54" x 75"
Queen	60" x 80"
King	76" x 80"
California King	72" x 84"

Most college dorm beds are long twins.

Beds on the Market

Here's some information that may make your decision easier:

❖ **The metal frame:** lightweight; inexpensive; fits in a car; easy to obtain and carry; quick to assemble with few or no tools. (If the one you buy doesn't have holes for a headboard, the bedding store has adapter kits to solve the problem.)

    One manufacturer makes an adjustable steel bed frame that comes in manageable-size boxes, is a snap to put together (without any tools), and—because of its height—negates the need for a box spring and leaves plenty of space underneath for storage.

❖ **The platform bed:** can be used with or without a box spring; available with built-in drawers or cubbies; comes with or without a headboard. There's a wide selection of styles and materials available, and most often need to be assembled in place.

❖ **The day bed:** sofa by day, bed by night; available with storage drawers; optional pullout trundle bed slides out from underneath the top mattress.

❖ **The captain's bed:** like a platform bed, but usually with extra headboard storage in addition to storage drawers or a trundle bed with casters underneath the mattress.

❖ **The futon:** available in a wide range of prices, frame materials, styles, and comfort levels; can be purchased assembled or not; extra features may include movable side arms, cup holders, and adjustable back and footrest; an enormous choice of covers is available for an instant change of style.

❖ **The Murphy bed:** this is the true hideaway bed; when it's put away, there's no clue that it even exists. (See below.)

Realty under the Bed

Beds are big, and so is the area beneath them. Strong plastic or wooden cups called **"bed risers" are a great way to maximize that space.** When placed under the frame feet, they lift the bed, allowing you to slide larger storage containers—and anything else you want to tuck away—in and out with ease. **Some bed frames come with built-in drawers underneath, which is a great way to make sure you're using every inch of under-the-bed storage.**

Quick Tip

Hide mismatched bins by using a dust ruffle. Today's versions aren't frilly and white—although those are still available, if you prefer. But many now sport modern colors and clean lines.

sweet dreams

Go to the Mattresses

No matter what kind of bed frame you choose, you'll also have to decide on the kind of mattress (and box spring) to go with it. The choices are so abundant, it's dizzying. There are different depths, filling materials, construction layers, fabric coverings, degrees of firmness, toppers (flat-top, pillow-top, foam-top), and so forth. If you can't decide, **go to a bedding store and try out the floor samples** until one of them feels just right.

Platform and **trundle beds are a huge convenience in kids' rooms, whether for slumber parties or visiting relatives.** If you're interested in either of them, you could buy a one-piece mattress and innerspring system that eliminates the need for a separate traditional box spring. This unusual combo comes vacuum packed in a box with wheels and will fit in the back seat of almost any car. Once opened and unsealed, it expands to full size. How great is that for moving?

Eating In

Any time you go shopping for a table, you're going to **consider style, price, and value.** But when your space is limited, you'll want to ask a few more questions: can this piece be used in more than one room? Can items be stored in it, above it, or beneath it? **Is it compact enough for every day, but expandable if company comes?** If you select a well-made multipurpose table, you'll be able to use it move after move, this year, next year, and five years down the road.

Illusions of Grandeur

Even if your current dining space is hardly bigger than a dinner napkin and it seems as though a tiny bistro table is the only thing that will fit, think about the future. **See whether you can find a table with the small surface size you need right now, but one that has hinged, drop-down, flip-open, or built-in (refractory style) leaves.** A table isn't always just a dining surface. If you look around a bit, you'll find not only some that have expansion and storage options but also many that have extra built-in goodies, such as drawers, shelves, or wine racks.

Create Extra Counter Space

Once you have a **counter-height island,** you'll wonder how you ever managed without it. **You can buy one or make your own by fastening a salvaged table top to a two-sided cabinet base.** You'll wind up with extra storage, an eating surface, and more prep space. If you add casters, it will be all set for the move to your next home, where it may leave the kitchen and play a new role in a craft or laundry room.

Quick Tip

Even a piece of plywood can become a working countertop with the help of a few self-adhesive vinyl tiles. Ones that mimic small ceramic tiles look the best when cut to fit.

Who couldn't use more counter space? **If your microwave is eating up too much of your work surface, you could mount it on a shelf over the stove to save space,** or purchase a microwave cart, which would add storage space, as well. That will give you more than enough room for a toaster and coffee pot. And if you look around, you can probably find one of those cool 3-in-1 appliances that combine a toaster oven, coffee maker, and griddle.

eating in

Find Unused Space

Why take up kitchen floor space unnecessarily? **Use the inside of a cabinet door to hold garbage bags or a mounted trash can.** How much room is there behind your kitchen sink? An inch? It can be a lot more than that with **a shelf that straddles the sink** and sits high enough to give you access to the faucets. Need more work space? **Some dish-draining racks are made to fit inside the sink,** which frees up a ton of countertop. There is an infinite variety of products available to make your kitchen work for you.

Study Solutions

If you haven't a room for a traditional office or study, or even a desk, you can still find areas to do some work on your laptop. If a couple of people want to check email or write a report at the same time, it's also convenient to have a secondary work space. Wall-mounted flip down desks and **narrow tower units are perfect answers.**

If you live in a place that has a lot of people coming and going, or even if you live alone, **it's always a good idea to have a couple of stash spots for valuables** such as electronic gadgets, jewelry, laptops, and mad money. There are fake books, soda cans, and picture frames on the market that are made for that purpose, but the simplest method is to have a desk with at least one section that locks.

Modular Offices

If you have a spacious area that you can designate for work or study, **explore modular office furniture.** It's an ideal choice for frequent movers. Besides the desk surface, there are open units, some with shelving, and others with closed cabinets. The sections can be moved easily so they fit against and atop one another in any arrangement you like. Because all the modular pieces don't have to conform to a given height, they are **great to use in spaces that have sloped ceilings or on walls with windows.** The building-block flexibility allows you to set up the furniture on a living room or office wall, and reconfigure it whenever you move again—and the pieces are attractive enough to be used in other rooms for other purposes. **Some manufactures make bookcases with a variety of fitted accessories—boxes, files, cabinet doors—so you can customize your office space to your needs.** These pieces can even be used as room dividers.

A Closet to Spare

Is it just a dream, or do you have a closet to spare? **You can convert a closet to prime office space by choosing a storage system that allows you to manipulate the components to suit your needs.** And if company drops in, you can leave it a bit of a mess and simply shut the door.

Build a Desk (Sort Of)

For a do-it-yourself project, nothing's easier than making a desk. **Start with two cabinets of the same size (file cabinets are ideal) and top them off with a length of laminated countertop.** You can also use a flush door or piece of plywood, which can be left natural, stained, varnished, or covered with stick-on floor tile.

For quick-access storage, use a desk hutch (below), or mount two or three shelves above the work area. Using baskets or boxes on the shelves will keep you totally organized. One can hold a camera and flash drives; another can be used for scissors, tape, and a stapler; and another can hold envelopes, stamps, and stationery.

In Plain Sight

It's also smart to have some kind of message board near the desk for reminders, bills coming due, or maybe photos that take your mind off of those bills. When you keep things out in the open rather than tucked away in a file, you're much more likely to remember them when you need them. If you're all business, **a corkboard is fine and functional and can be embellished to complement the room;** if you want to have something that's both functional and stylish, a memory board will do the trick. It's a dynamite way to add texture, color, and function. A memory board is lightweight and can hold everything from photos and to-do lists to takeout menus. You don't need tacks or pushpins because items are just slipped beneath crisscrossed elastic cords or ribbons. (See page 114.) Placing two or three together looks like wall art.

Making a Memory Board

DECORATING KIT

- ❖ Measuring tape
- ❖ Scissors
- ❖ Corkboard or foam core board
- ❖ Cotton batting
- ❖ Fabric
- ❖ Coordinated ribbon or elastic
- ❖ Buttons
- ❖ Staple gun
- ❖ Glue

Making your own memory board is fun, simple, and inexpensive. All you need is a flat board or a piece of foam core.

1. Measure the board. Cut a piece of cotton batting that is large enough to cover the front and wrap around the back of the board, where you will staple it.
2. Cover the batting with the fabric, wrapping it around to the back and attaching it using staples. For a neat look, miter the corners.
3. Measure and cut lengths of ribbon or elastic; the number will depend on the size of your board.
4. Arrange the ribbons in a pattern, such as straight, evenly spaced vertical or diagonal rows followed by straight, evenly spaced horizontal or opposite diagonal rows.
5. Attach the ribbons to the board using staples wherever they overlap. Cover the staples with buttons, glued in place.

study solutions

Message Central

If you're sharing digs, it's really important to communicate, so hang a dry-erase or cork bulletin board—and get into the habit of really using it. It's a good way to relay messages to your roomies. You know, info you don't want them to miss, such as "your mom called," "the landlord is coming," or "classes are canceled!"

How about a new take on pegboard? Remember when pegboard was only used in the garage or basement? Not any more. **Pegboard is inexpensive, can be painted any color, and can be used in any room—especially offices, playrooms, kitchens, and kids' rooms.** You can use it to post notes, organize untensils, or hang baskets and bins that keep toys off of the floor. In order to enjoy its

full potential and make use of the many attachable plastic-coated hooks and colorful baskets that are available, **pegboard needs to be a tiny bit away from the wall.** All you need to do is screw a couple of thin furring strips to the wall; then screw the pegboard to the strips. This will allow enough space for the hooks to be slipped in and out of the holes easily.

chapter 5

Ordinary to Extraordinary

Do you have a mix of new and old furnishings, but crave a coordinated look? Find out how to use what you already have and buy what you need for less money. After deciding on what you want, adding charm, personality, and function is only a short stroll away. In hardly any time at all you can give your new place designer flair with simple projects and a few clever tips for pulling everything together. Making carefree improvements has never been easier. You'll find satisfaction every step of the way, and have some fun while you're at it. So take a quick look around to see what you have to renovate. You'll be surprised by what you can do.

Skimp or Splurge

Even with a modest budget, it's possible to purchase new furniture that's built to last. You just have to know where to look, and **avoid buying poorly made pieces that might fall apart after a couple of moves.** In many retail shops, you can find "as is" floor models for a fraction of their original price—and really, do you care if that lovely console table has a tiny ding on the side you never see? Besides, it's already assembled.

Many high-end retail stores have **discount outlet centers,** and numerous furniture manufacturers have factory outlets, too. Pay them a visit, and you might be able to snatch up some amazing bargains. Bottom line: **if you're going to splurge on a piece of furniture, ask yourself whether it's something you want to have for a long time.** If not, keep on walking. Keep in mind, too, that antique and vintage furnishings not only have aesthetic worth, but they might appreciate in value.

Buried Treasure

Treasure hunting is a good way to spend free time: you can get new ideas, fresh air, and exercise all at the same time. Explore antique shops, flea markets, thrift stores, and yard sales. Just remember to wear comfortable footwear and to resist being overly tempted by the array of unique items. There will be lots of "finds" that are lovely just the way they are, but besides considering how much you like a piece, think about what characteristics are most important to you. **If the alluring object isn't in perfect shape, ask yourself whether it has "good bones."** Is it at least in working condition? If not, what will it take to make it function well and look great again? Is it something you can repair, repaint, or re-cover yourself? Those are the practical things you need to think about. But sometimes **you may see something that ignites your imagination.**

Window Frames

A great flea-market find is a charming paned window. A window frame can become a multi-sectioned frame for your favorite photos, a dramatic way of displaying vintage magazine covers, or a showcase for drawings, postcards, or perhaps old maps. You can hang it vertically or horizontally, and even add hooks to hold favorite collections. **Make your space seem much larger by attaching a mirror to a window frame that's lost its glass. Then place the whole thing opposite a real window.** Top it off with simple curtains on a rod, and you'll be amazed at how bright and sunny your room looks with its new "double exposure."

Repaint & Refinish

You did it—you found some yard-sale treasures. A critical look tells you that it's time to spruce them up, along with your old favorites and hand-me-downs. With a little creative TLC you can extend the life of secondhand furniture for years. **Refinishing is easy, economical, and satisfying, and it's far greener to re-do than to toss.** With a selection of quick-hold glues, fast-drying paints, and premade trim, sprucing up furniture and home decor items has never been easier.

Are you the instant-gratification type? If so, **go the spray-paint route.** There's a huge array of colors from which to choose, including **gorgeous metallics for a distinctive touch.** All you'll need is a well-ventilated area, a drop cloth, and the spray paint. In minutes, your old item will have a brand-new finish. By repainting your old lamps, a couple of picture frames, and a large vase, **you can transform an outdated look to one with real sizzle—and in exactly the color you want.**

Quick Tip

Using accent pieces in a coordinating hue and placing them at different heights throughout the room will add a designer's touch.

Paint Effects

If you enjoy creative crafts and have a couple of hours to indulge, consider using stain or a faux finish kit. **Beyond a basic change of color, you can achieve an entirely different finish.** You can enhance a piece of furniture or an accessory using materials that give the appearance of stone, metal, or even leather. **If you'd prefer to make your project piece look like it's been loved for a century or two, you can give it a distressed or weathered look, or an antique, crackled, or pickled finish.** Don't be surprised when your friends ask, "When did you get that?"

Applying a Crackle Glaze

DECORATING KIT

- Acrylic paint for base coat
- Acrylic paint for top coat
- Crackle medium
- Antiquing medium
- Paintbrushes
- Soft lint-free cloth

How about trying an antique crackled finish? It makes each piece look as though it has a history and works beautifully on old tables, dressers, chairs, and frames.

1. Apply two coats of the base color, and let it dry.

2. Using a clean brush, make one pass with the crackle medium over the entire surface. The thicker the coat, the wider the cracks will be. Do not go over the same area twice.

3. When the crackle medium is almost, but not completely dry, apply a contrasting top coat.

4. After the top coat curls back to reveal the base-coat color, rub the antiquing medium over the cracks using a soft rag.

5. Allow the project to cure for at least 24 hours; then apply the sealer, and let it dry.

Make It Look Old Again

Sometimes a piece of furniture works well, but looks like it should be retired. It's nicked, scuffed, scraped, and gouged; but it has great deep drawers, and you don't want to part with it. **If you want to change that eyesore into an eye-catcher, turn its imperfections into a plus.** Go with it—add even more dents and scrapes; restain it; and seal it with a clear satin finish. Presto—you have a professional distressed look.

Another playful approach is decoupage. Using decoupage medium, apply a collection of images or fabric cuttings that have special meaning to you, and finish with a clear varnish (inset below). You'll wind up with a fantastic conversation piece that's on its way to becoming a treasured heirloom.

Wood: A Second Skin

If you own a wooden piece that's lost its sheen, before considering chemical stripping, sanding, stain, or paint, try giving it a "spa treatment." **Think of wood, a natural material, as similar to your skin.** If you keep it clean, moisturized, and protected, it will look better for a longer time. And just like skin, wood can become dry. It has a thirst for minerals and oils. **Wood conditioners can make a huge difference** in the appearance of furniture. **Like good facial products, they'll minimize flaws and protect the surface from damaging elements.**

Sometimes, all an old wooden piece really needs is a good drink. Amazingly, **wood can be revived in a matter of 10 to 15 minutes. It just takes a clean rag, a natural oil—such as linseed, almond, or even olive oil— and a little elbow grease.** For items with years of built-up dirt, such as a banister, douse some oil on extra-fine steel wool; rub the area gently; and then wipe off any residue. In moments, you'll see unbelievable results that will last a year or more.

repaint & refinish

Quick Tip

How often you need to recondition wooden furniture depends on the climate. If you live in a dry area, you'll need to do it more often.

Cover-Ups

Not everyone is game for refinishing an old dresser or table, but that doesn't mean you can't give it a lift. You'd be surprised by what can be done without glue or paint.

For a sturdy table that doesn't have anything going for it but a flat surface, **a floor-length fabric topper is a fast and effortless way to make it useful and attractive.** You'll gain a little hidden storage while completely disguising the less-than-lovely table beneath its folds. Furthermore, the **fabric adds another bit of color, texture, and elegance.** To make it a snap to keep clean, top the surface with a piece of glass that's been cut to the same size.

Top It Off

Many furniture items really only need help on the top surface. That's what usually gets most of the stains, burns, and scratches, while the rest of the piece stays looking pretty good. If that's the case, **try covering the top with a hard material, such as mirror, marble, slate, or ceramic tile.** No need for coasters; these materials are resistant to water, burns, and stains. **Self-adhesive cork, vinyl squares, and faux copper or tin tiles** are more quick fixes that can be used on cabinet door fronts and sides as well as the tops.

Furniture Rehab

There are so many clever, inexpensive ways to rehabilitate furnishings that you may have a hard time choosing just one. You'll not only find ways to **make things look new and beautiful** again, you'll be able to **change their style in minutes.** Here are just a few effective methods:

❖ Wind hemp or another textured fiber around lamp bases or furniture legs to add a natural element and, at the same time, hide imperfections.

❖ Update hardware, such as knobs, handles, drawer pulls, and wood trim, to change a cabinet or dresser front dramatically.

❖ Use your stitching skills to embroider a purchased pattern onto a lampshade, pillowcase, or throw.

❖ Add thin strips of veneer or molding to dress up cabinets.

❖ For a high-tech look, have a thin piece of sheet metal cut about ⅛ in. smaller than the surface size (to avoid sharp edges), and glue it in place.

❖ Dress up a lampshade using stencils, fabric trim, or colorful stick-on embellishments.

cover-ups

How to Make Over a Paper Lampshade

DECORATING KIT

- Old or new paper lampshade
- Kraft paper ✤ Pencil ✤ Scissors
- Paper clip ✤ Spray adhesive
- Fabric, wallpaper, or decorative paper
- Fabric trim or beads (optional)
- Glue gun

1. Create a template. Place the shade on a large sheet of kraft paper, and then roll it, tracing the top and bottom edges as you go.

2. Cut out the template after you've completed tracing the diameter of both the top and bottom of the shade.

3. Fit the pattern around the lampshade, and secure it with a paper clip; then make necessary adjustments, such as trimming away any excess.

4. Trace this pattern onto the wrong side of the fabric, wallpaper, or decorative paper; then cut, following the outline.

5. Spray the back of the cutout with the adhesive, and then place it right side up on the shade, smoothing as you go.

6. For an optional finishing flourish, glue beaded, tasseled, corded, or braided trim to the bottom of the shade.

The Biggest Cover-Up

Do you need to save your sofa? Is it sagging and faded? Does it no longer suit your style? First, make it comfortable; have your local home improvement store cut a piece of fiberboard or plywood to size (which is done at no charge), and put it under the seat cushions. If your cushion covers have zippers, get in there and plump them up with fiberfill. Then comes the fun part—choosing a slipcover. **The selection of slipcovers is enormous.** They're made in a rainbow of colors, patterns, textures, styles, and prices. And they're **the easiest way to change the look of your living room.** Solid colors are always a safe choice because they make it easier to change your color scheme later. Save the patterns for pillows and throws that you can change in a flash.

Before buying a slipcover, take a look at its cleaning instructions. **Machine-washable fabrics are easier to maintain than the ones that say "dry clean only."** Fabrics that are 100 percent cotton have a tendency to shrink and fade more easily than synthetics, which are more resistant to spills and sunlight. Once you put a slipcover on a chair or sofa, you can **use a spray-on stain repellant for extra protection against soiling.** These sprays have a long shelf life and can also be used on suede or fabric shoes, coats, purses, and even car interiors.

Quick Tip

Furniture stores can order replacement cushions for most sofas, loveseats, and chairs. The brand or model doesn't matter—it's the size that counts.

Repurpose & Reuse

It's not only furniture that can be resurrected. You can also repurpose smaller household items, so give them a little thought before tossing them. **Did you ever receive a gift basket and wonder what to do with it after the goodies were gone?** Small ones make neat places to keep napkins, mail, or remote controls, and **larger ones can hold rolled-up towels in the bathroom or act as a cleaning-supply caddy.** A basket's natural material makes it an attractive addition wherever you use it.

Everyday Things

Finished with that jar of raspberry jam? **Before putting it in the recycle bin, think about it. In a matter of minutes, you could probably come up with 10 ways to make that jar an asset.** The number of everyday grocery items that are packaged in reusable containers is mind-boggling. Many have easy-to-remove labels, and what's more, they usually have good lids. Often that **leaves you with brightly colored storage containers** that you can jazz up or use just as they are. If you want to decorate them, paint them, use stick-on embellishments found at craft stores, cover them with contact paper, or just add strips of colored vinyl tape. **So the next time you finish the coffee, frosting, or margarine, save the tubs and jars.** These vessels are perfect for storing leftover food or acting as planters or flower vases, and they also make first-rate catchalls for holding hair accessories, desk supplies, and hardware. Besides organizing your space, they'll add a punch of color—and they're already packed for your next move.

Quick Tip

If you save three or four identical sealable containers, you'll have a set of unbreakable, air-tight canisters for spices, coffee beans, or baking necessities.

What Is Upcycling?

Upcycling is making better use of something that's disposable. Some of the things that first come to mind are old muffin and cupcake tins, cracked flowerpots, flatware trays, and jars of all sizes. There are slews of uses you can find for these items, but here are a few others with potential for your consideration:

❖ Mismatched wine glasses can be decorative upside down or right side up. If you stand one on its rim, the base can hold a pillar candle. Or place a few mismatched glasses on a mantle or coffee table holding decorative elements that complement the decor of the room.

❖ Wine corks can be used to prop up your laptop. Placing two corks under the base at the back will keep it at a comfortable angle and reduce heat build-up.

❖ Corks can also fill a bowl or vase for a decorative touch, or they can be sliced into disks and placed under furniture feet for easier, scratch-free movement.

❖ Anything can be decorative when placed in an inexpensive bowl or vase, including cotton balls in the bathroom, citrus rinds in the kitchen—which have the bonus of smelling good—and torn-out magazine articles in the living room. This also puts your vases to good use when they're not holding flowers.

❖ Speaking of citrus, you can decorate with fruit for an organic look by placing it in bowls or baskets. Use whatever kind of fruit has the color that complements your decor. (Plus you can steal one when you're hungry.) Using fruit of the same color makes a stronger statement.

- The cardboard tubes left after finishing rolls of paper towels, gift wrap, foil, and plastic wrap can become safe storage for items that might otherwise be damaged while being moved or stuffed into a drawer or closet.
- Plastic pill vials are perfect for storing sewing needles, beads, and other tiny notions. They're also a good way to carry small jewelry pieces when traveling.
- Cardboard egg cartons make excellent "wells" for starting seeds; the foam kind make good paint palettes; and both can morph into junk-drawer organizers for holding paper clips, pushpins, tacks, and other small things.
- Large plastic bottles with handles, such as the ones used for milk and laundry liquids, become ideal funnels. After thoroughly cleaning one, cut off some of the bottom. Once you remove the cap and turn it upside down, you can use it for adding fluids to your car, filling a bird feeder, or anything else you want to pour without a spill.

- For any size plastic bottle with a handle, here's the scoop: leave the cap on and, starting above the handle, cut the bottom off diagonally. Use it to scoop pet chow, flour, birdseed, or potting soil.
- Don't discard upright file-folder holders; use them to organize pot lids.
- Let a medium-size plastic storage box double as a nightstand that doesn't take up extra space. Just put a piece of wood—cut to size—over the top, and throw a floor-length table-cloth over it.

Make a Cat Scratch Pad

DECORATING KIT

- ✤ Cardboard boxes
- ✤ Sharp scissors or utility knife
- ✤ Masking tape
- ✤ Duct tape

Do you have more cardboard boxes than you can fit in your recycle bin? Do you also have a cat? Here's an easy project that your furry friend will love—and that will keep him away from all of your new furniture. Cats are playful creatures, and if you don't give them something, they'll find a "toy" on their own. Scratch pads fill an instinctual need to scratch and to sharpen their claws. Here's an easy way to make one using all those extra cardboard boxes.

1. Cut a couple of flattened cartons into 3-in. strips.

2. Wind one strip into a tight coil.

3. Attach the next strip, short end to short end, with some masking tape on each side, and keep winding.

4. When it's large enough, use some duct tape on the underside to help hold everything together; it will look like an oversized round placemat.

5. Sprinkle the pad with a little catnip for a purr-fectly fantastic scratching pad.

Choose to Reuse

You don't need to take out an ad or send a blanket email to spread the word. By using and displaying your repurposed items, you're sending a clear, caring message to your friends and visitors that green is the way to go. **In addition to reusing items, you can purchase beautiful organic furnishings for your home.** Add it all up, and you'll probably have the lowest carbon footprint on your block.

chapter 6

Movin' On

Thinking about your upcoming
move and all the things you need
to prepare can be overwhelming, but
with a good plan and a little head start
you can make the process of coming and going
a whole lot easier.

Really, a move can be a reason to celebrate; say goodbye
to things you won't miss—such as the window that sticks,
the cupboard that doesn't quite close, and the faucet that
hiccups. Focus on the positives. You can look forward to a
clean slate, a chance to make your new home even more
comfortable and attractive, and the fun of exploring your
new community.

So put on some music, pack, and dance, and then dance
some more. You'll be amazed by how easy it is to accomplish it all.

Prep Like a Pro

It may not be your first move, and it probably won't be your last, but what's important is making it go as smoothly as possible. The challenge, of course, is coordinating what seems like hundreds of little details. The way to handle them is by using the same method you'd use if you were organizing a wedding or starting a small business: **make a list and a plan, and stick to them.** Whether it's across the country, across town, or across the street, **smart planning can turn a potentially high-stress transition into an exciting new adventure.**

Quick Tip

Keep your old phone book, and be sure to request a new one when arranging for your new land-line service. You might want the name of a good take-out place for that first night.

Hammer Out the Details

Get the pesky details out of the way before you start packing.

* ❖ Check your rental agreement. If it calls for giving ample notice to your landlord, do it in writing and send it certified mail or with a delivery-confirmation receipt.

* ❖ Talk to all your utility providers about shutoff and turn-on dates at your new place.

* ❖ Pick up a free change of address kit at the post office to let all your friends and family members know when and where you're moving.

* ❖ Notify your doctor, pharmacy, insurance, bank, credit card companies, magazine subscriptions, and the like.

You can get through all of the above in a couple of hours, easy. In fact, these days, you can do most, if not all, of this online—you can even change the address on your driver's license this way. Just go right down your must-do list, and before you know it, everything will be crossed off as completed.

Get to Know the Neighborhood

If your new home isn't too far away, **do a dry run through the neighborhood.** Figure out the commuting time to work or school; find out the locations of the supermarket, drug store, gas station, and library. **It will build a sense of familiarity and smooth the transition.**

Prep like a pro

Make Arrangements for Pets

Do you have a pet? **Make arrangements ahead of time** to have it stay with a friend or neighbor while furniture and cartons are being taken out of your place. **Cats and dogs don't like their routines disrupted,** and all the unusual activity stresses out even the most laid-back ones. There's also the danger of doors left open, and the last thing you want to do is frantically search the neighborhood for a missing pet during an already hectic time.

Think about Transportation...

For the physical move, you can **search online for moving companies, see what options they offer, and arrange for free estimates.** Once you decide which one you want, book the moving date in advance so you won't have any last-minute surcharges or headaches. **If you're planning a casual DIY move with a rental truck and some buddies, reserve it for the time you need,** and let your friends know the date as soon as you know what it is. Just remember, pizza and beer go a long way toward creating good will among prospective moving helpers.

Quick Tip

If you have a collection of prized and fragile items— Grandma's heirloom glass ornaments, or just like-colored pieces you've picked up at yard sales over the years—be safe and pack it yourself.

...and Packing Materials

Check your supplies well ahead of time. You may have to buy packing tape, markers, and a few bungee cords, but you can get nearly everything else absolutely free. Most home improvement centers will give you tailgate flags, and if you go to a local furniture store and carpet warehouse, you'll hit the mother lode. That's where you can get used bubble wrap, foam board, and scraps of new carpet padding for protecting furniture. (You can also feel good about reusing them.) Mostly, **you'll need cartons**—which can be pricey to buy—**so stop in at your local supermarkets, liquor stores, and office-supply shops.** They all have special days when they unload their orders and have plenty of cartons available. Ask nicely, and you shall receive.

Prep like a pro

Be Specific

Begin packing up about two weeks before moving day—a month if you have a ton of stuff. If you pack a few cartons every night or so, the last few days will seem much less hectic. Start with all the out-of-season clothing and the household items you seldom use.

Try not to be vague when labeling the cartons. **A box that just says "kitchen stuff" may tell the movers where to put it, but it won't help you locate the coffeemaker when you need your caffeine fix.** Write the contents on the side of each carton, and the room where it belongs on top of the carton, and your unpacking time will be cut in half. **Brightly mark a couple of "fast-find" cartons for sentimental items and important papers.** Another group of items to keep together and handy should include a first-aid kit, fire extinguisher, and a crank-operated flashlight. This "safety box" should be the last thing packed and the first thing unpacked.

Once again, you have the opportunity to pare down items that don't work or you simply don't want anymore. Better to donate those things sooner than later. Why bother hauling them somewhere else?

Quick Fixes

Once everything is off the walls, go room to room and **fill any depressions, scrapes, and nail or screw holes with joint compound.** If you're careful not to overfill, you'll barely need to sand them later. If you accidentally made a large hole, such as one caused by a door knob, pick up a home repair wall-patch kit. It's easy to use and fast drying. Or check out "Fixing Small Holes," below, and "Fixing Large Holes," on the following page.

Fixing Small Holes

DECORATING KIT

❖ Taping knife
❖ Sandpaper
❖ Patching material
❖ Joint compound

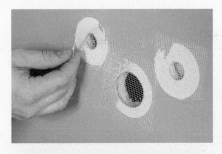

1. You can plug small openings with screening, or apply surface mesh to support and reinforce repair compound.

2. Instead of falling into the hole, joint compound embeds in the mesh. Multiple coats are needed to create a smooth surface.

Over larger holes, use a self-sticking patch kit that has a reinforcing panel. Just peel off the backing, and apply. Once the mesh is fixed to the wall, spread joint compound over the entire patch; then sand, prime, and paint.

Fixing Large Holes

Small holes are easy to fix by just filling the spots with joint compound, letting it dry, and sanding it smooth. But larger holes require a bit more effort. You can either buy a "clip kit," or you can use scrap lumber, construction adhesive, and a drywall scrap that's large enough to cover the hole. A little tip: square up the hole before you make the patch. This makes following the steps a lot easier.

DECORATING KIT

- Drywall saw or utility knife
- Caulking gun
- Power drill/driver or hammer
- 6-in. taping knife
- Sanding sponge
- Drywall patch
- 1x3 scraps or furring
- Drywall nails or screws
- Joint compound
- Construction adhesive

1. Cut out the damaged area, leaving a clean-edged rectangular shape. Cut 1x3 braces to fasten inside the new cutout.

2. Set the braces using construction adhesive and drywall screws. Hold or clamp the brace as you drive the screws.

3. Apply construction adhesive to the side braces before setting the patch. Add top and bottom braces on larger holes.

4. Place the patch piece on the braces; move it back and forth to set in the adhesive; and secure it using drywall screws.

5. Finish the seams of the patch with drywall tape (either paper or fiberglass) and three coats of joint compound.

6. Finish-sand the final coat using a small-celled sanding sponge. Prime the fresh compound before repainting the wall.

Use a Fresh Coat of Paint

If your landlord left you the remains of the last paint job, use it to finish your wall repairs. Otherwise, take a tiny flake of the paint to a home improvement store. They will scan and generate an exact match in a small quantity. For really tiny areas that need a touch-up, **a set of acrylic paints** (the kind found in craft shops) will have what you need for the job.

Quick Tip

Thoroughly prepare the site for painting using drop cloths and painter's tape. Prepare yourself by rubbing moisturizer on your hands and arms; paint will wash off more easily. Oh, and wear a hat!

quick fixes

Wood Floor Fixes

Little nicks and scuffs on woodwork or floors can disappear with a light dab of shoe polish, vegetable oil, or wood touch-up "crayons" or markers; they come in oak, cherry, walnut, and other wood tones. But **if the whole floor needs TLC, you can make it look great again by using quick-drying, one-step, clean-and-shine products** that can be found at any supermarket. After thoroughly vacuuming the floor, squirt on the cleaner and spread it evenly over the surface using a sponge mop. In minutes, your floors will look terrific; and all of those **little imperfections will have vanished.** For scuffed, dull, or dirty wood trim, turn to the same product, using a small damp sponge to apply it.

Carpet Fixes

If you accidentally spilled or spattered paint on the carpet during your touch-up, don't panic, and **don't make it worse by rubbing the dribble in deeper.** Instead, **carefully scoop, scrape, or blot up as much of the mess as you can.** Immediately afterward, use a clean rag sprayed with glass cleaner or fabric-stain remover to get rid of the remaining residue.

You know those **crushed areas of carpet** left by furniture legs? They can be fluffed up again by misting them with a little water and then using a blow dryer and a hair comb or brush. (Because some fibers can melt, don't use a hot setting or hold the dryer too close.) To avoid the problem in the future, **place small pieces of scrap carpeting face down under each furniture leg.**

Quick Tip

To minimize water rings on wood tables or floors, dip the corner of a clean, dry rag into a bit of vegetable oil, then into ashes, and rub it over the ring. Wipe it again with a clean, dry area of the cloth, and polish it normally.

Spot-Patching a Carpet

DECORATING KIT

- ❖ Carpet patch tool
- ❖ Carpet remnant
- ❖ Adhesive
- ❖ Double-faced seam tape

1. Use a circular carpet-patch tool to remove a cookie-cutter section around a deep stain, burn, or tear.

2. Peel the cover tape from a piece of double-faced tape. Cut it larger than the hole, and fold to insert.

3. Use the circular cutter to cut a patch piece from a remnant, and press it firmly in place over the adhesive.

Odor Solutions

You don't want the place to smell like a dog lived there, however subtle the scent is. **Pet stores have inexpensive solutions containing natural enzymes that will eliminate stains and odors quickly and effectively.** These products are wonderful to use when you want to leave your old place smelling fresh, and good to have on hand if you inherit any pet aromas in the new place. It's a way to avoid problems coming and going.

Even a clean apartment can smell a little stale if nobody's around to air it out. **A little "do unto others" consideration would be welcomed by the next occupants,** so leave a fresh, opened box of baking soda in the fridge, another on the kitchen counter, and even one in the bathroom. It's best not to try to mask odors with a fragrance, especially one that may contain harmful chemicals. Baking soda will absorb odors and leave rooms smelling fresh—naturally.

quick fixes

Natural Remedies

Fix what you've done with what you have on hand. Here are some tips for using everyday household items for quick fixes.

❖ Use equal parts lemon and water, and drip on tea-stained fabric. Rinse with water.

❖ Clean mirrors using newspaper and a mixture of one cup of distilled white vinegar and one cup of water for a streak-free surface.

❖ Spray cooking oil on squeaky hinges and sliding doors that stick.

❖ Use olive oil to shine stainless steel.

❖ Rub a dryer sheet over fabric to pick up pet hair.

❖ Use coffee filters between plates when packing.

❖ Run the dishwasher empty with a cup of vinegar to reduce grime build-up.

❖ To erase crayon, pencil, ink, and furniture scuffs from painted surfaces, sprinkle club soda on a damp sponge; blot the spot thoroughly; and rinse.

❖ To remove chewing gum or wax from fabric, gently rub the gunk with a zip-close bag filled with ice cubes until the substance hardens. Shatter gum with a blunt object; then vacuum up the chips. Carefully peel off frozen wax with a plastic spatula.

❖ Use undiluted distilled white vinegar to clean greasy kitchen surfaces.

❖ Wipe down walls using undiluted distilled white vinegar on a cloth to get rid of mildew and dust.

❖ Remove stains on upholstered furniture by rubbing undiluted distilled white vinegar directly onto the stain before washing it according to manufacturer instructions.

❖ For stains on plastic laminate, leave freshly squeezed lemon juice on the spot for half an hour; sprinkle it with baking soda; scrub; and then rinse.

Cleaning Top to Bottom

After the repairs are finished, start cleaning. It may not be your favorite chore, but do it thoroughly anyway, because getting your deposit back may depend on how well you do it. Ask your landlord for a copy of his move-out inspection list. This will be your "cheat-sheet" as to what you should be focusing on.

"Top to bottom" isn't just a cute phrase. You should literally clean your place starting at the top and working your way down to the bottom. All of the dust and dirt will make its way to the floor, which would be the last place you clean. Clean like you've just committed a crime—don't leave any forensic evidence.

Here's a sample move-out cleaning checklist to help you along.

KITCHEN
❖ **Stove/Oven**
- ❑ All outer surfaces (including sides)
- ❑ Under, behind, and around unit
- ❑ Burners and surface beneath burners
- ❑ Inside, including racks and broiler drawer

❖ **Refrigerator**
- ❑ All outer surfaces (including sides and top)
- ❑ Under, behind, and around unit
- ❑ Evaporation coil (which attracts lint and hair)
- ❑ Inside: remove all shelves and drawers; each piece should be cleaned individually.
- ❑ The freezer

❖ **Counters/Cabinets**
- ❑ Inside cabinets and drawers
- ❑ All visible surfaces
- ❑ Top of cabinets

❖ **Dishwasher**
- ❑ Inside
- ❑ Front surface

❖ Sink(s)
- ❑ All surfaces ("erasing" scrubbers come in handy)
- ❑ Clean and polish faucet and knobs/handles.

BATHROOM
- ❑ Shower, tub, sink(s), and toilet (every tangible part): use a bathroom-specific cleanser. For added sparkle, scrape off old, mildewed caulk, and then run a fresh bead of caulking around the edge of the tub.
- ❑ Mirror(s): use mirror-cleaning solution. (See page 155.)
- ❑ Medicine cabinet: inside and out
- ❑ Fixtures: clean and polish, removing all mildew and mold
- ❑ Cabinets, drawers, countertops: all visible surfaces and all interiors.

WALLS
- ❑ Remove all cobwebs.
- ❑ Wipe down surface.
- ❑ Repair and paint over damaged areas.
- ❑ If you smoked inside, you may have to repaint all walls.

FLOORING
- ❑ Sweep all bare floors using a broom and a dustpan.
- ❑ Vacuum all floors, including those you swept.
- ❑ Mop linoleum or tile floors; clean hardwood floors, using a wood-floor product.
- ❑ Remove stains from carpeting; steam clean if necessary. (If your carpets are just lightly soiled, the stains should vanish if you use spray-on foam cleanser. If they're a mess, rent a carpet-cleaning machine or hire a service.)

GENERAL
- ❑ Throughout: dust everything, especially light fixtures and shades, trimwork, radiators, and ceiling fans.
- ❑ Windows: sills, trim, tracks, sash, glass (inside and out), curtain rods; replace or patch screens if there are holes.
- ❑ Blinds, curtains: dismount and soak blinds in a bathtub to clean thoroughly; hand-wash and dry curtains and drapes.

Grand Finale

Twenty-four hours to go? **Pack a suitcase with a change or two of clothes, pajamas, and toiletries** (including the ibuprofen), as well as your old phone book, laptop and charger, and whatever else you need on a daily basis. **Get a jump start by disassembling any furniture you can to make more space in the van.**

If you've swapped overhead light fixtures, remove yours and put back the original ones. The same goes for the showerhead, switch plates, blinds, et cetera. **Put everything back the way you found it.** This is the time to take out the pictures you took on the first day and compare. Does the place look great? Even better than when you arrived? **Take a photo.** You may not need it, but if there's a legal dispute, it's the tool that can help you get back your security deposit.

Home, Sweet Home

Everything's done. The cartons and furniture are in the van, and in just a few hours a whole new adventure will begin—new rooms, new neighbors, and new friends. You'll be able to find your coffee pot in a New York minute, and **before you know it, you'll get into a comfortable routine.** You'll know all the best take-out places, what day the trash is picked up, and what time the mail comes. By the end of the first week, the cupboards, fridge, and hamper will start to fill, the floor will need its first mopping, and **your new place will truly feel like home.**

The End

resources

The following list of manufacturers, retailers, and associations is meant to be a general guide to additional industry and product-related sources. It is not intended as a listing of products and manufacturers represented by the photographs in this book.

manufacturers & retailers

Ace
www.acehardware.com
Sells home-improvement and decor items.

Armstrong
717-397-0611
www.armstrong.com
Manufactures ceilings, cabinets, and floors, including laminate flooring systems.

Ballard
800-536-7551
www.ballarddesigns.com
Online retail source for home furnishings.

Bed in a Box
800-588-5720
www.bedinabox.com
Manufactures memory-foam mattresses that are compressed into manageable boxes for delivery; they expand when removed.

Benjamin Moore
800-344-0400
www.benjaminmoore.com
Manufactures paint, varnishes, and related products.

Blik Surface Graphics
866-262-2545
www.whatisblik.com
Manufactures self-adhesive, removable wall decals in a variety of sizes, colors, and styles.

Container Store
800-266-8246
www.containerstore.com
Sells customizable closet systems and myriad organizational products.

Country Curtains

800-456-0321

www.countrycurtains.com

A national retailer and online source for ready-made curtains, draperies, shades, blinds, hardware, and accessories.

Designer Rods

www.designerrods.com

Manufactures decorative towel rods filled with colorful sea glass, shells, or marbles.

Easy Closets

800-910-0129

www.easyclosets.com

Manufactures closet systems.

Elfa

www.elfa.com

Manufactures storage products.

EZ Moves

800-847-4683

www.ezmoves.com

Manufactures furniture slides for both hard and soft surfaces.

Forbo

866-MARMOLEUM

www.forboflooringna.com

Manufactures environmentally friendly, hygienic, and flexible flooring solutions.

Hunter Douglas

800-789-0331

www.hunterdouglas.com

Manufactures window treatments and systems.

IKEA

www.ikea.com

Sells functional, affordable, and innovative home furnishings.

Improvements Catalog

800-634-9484

www.improvementscatalog.com

Sells unique products meant to solve decorative, organizational, and functional problems around the house.

resources

Kraftmaid Cabinetry
440-632-5333
www.kraftmaid.com
Manufactures cabinetry.

Manhattan Cabinetry
800-626-4288
www.manhattancabinetry.com
Manufactures Murphy beds.

Merillat
www.merillat.com
Manufactures cabinetry and accessories.

Modern Wall Graphics
888-259-5767
www.modernwallgraphics.com
Manufactures removable vinyl wall decals
in a large variety of sizes, colors, and styles.

Mohawk Industries, Inc.
800-266-4295
www.mohawkflooring.com
Manufactures carpeting, area rugs, hardwood,
laminate, ceramic tile, and vinyl flooring.

ORG
800-562-4257
www.homeorg.com
Manufactures home-organization systems
and solutions.

RoomMates
800-236-4520
www.roommatespeelandstick.com
Manufactures self-adhesive, removable wall
decals in a variety of sizes, colors, and styles.

Rust-Oleum
800-323-3584
www.rustoleum.com
Manufactures paint and faux-finish products,
including frosted-glass spray.

Sherwin Williams
www.sherwinwilliams.com
Manufactures paint and finishes.

Shower Bridge
www.showerbridge.com
Manufactures a storage unit that fits in the
open space over your shower.

Stacks and Stacks
800-761-5222
www.stacksandstacks.com
Manufactures storage and organization
products.

resources

Sure-Fit, Inc.
888-796-0500
www.surefit.net
Manufactures ready-made slipcovers.

Target
www.target.com
Sells home furnishing and organizational products, such as Huggable Hangers and Space Bags.

Thibaut, Inc.
800-223-0704
www.thibautdesign.com
Manufactures coordinating wallpaper and fabrics.

Viva Terra
800-233-6011
www.vivaterra.com
Manufactures organic, sustainable, and handcrafted home furnishings.

WalMart
www.walmart.com
Sells home furnishings and organizational products, including the SmartBase steel bed frame.

York Wallcoverings
717-846-4456
www.yorkwall.com
Manufactures borders and wallcoverings.

The Freecycle Network
www.freecycle.org
A private, nonprofit organization whose members exchange used items rather than discard them.

Goodwill Industries International
800-741-0186
www.goodwill.org
A nonprofit membership organization that provides education, training, and career services for people with disadvantages. The revenues from clothing and household goods donated and sold at Goodwill stores nationwide fund the organization's services.

Green People
732-514-1066
www.greenpeople.org
An online directory of eco-friendly products, services, organizations, and events.

Green Seal
202-872-6400
www.greenseal.org
An independent nonprofit organization that promotes the manufacture, purchase, and use of environmentally responsible products and services. The Green Seal identifies a product as environmentally preferable.

Habitat for Humanity International

800-422-4828

www.habitat.org

A nonprofit, ecumenical Christian housing ministry that seeks to eliminate poverty housing and homelessness. Volunteers help build houses around the world for families in need.

OrganizedHome.com

www.organizedhome.com

An online forum that offers advice to consumers about home organization.

The Salvation Army

www.salvationarmyusa.org

A nonprofit organization well known for its charitable efforts and social services, including disaster relief. The sale of donated items at Salvation Army thrift stores goes to support the organization's addiction-recovery program.

The Surface Store

www.thesurfacestore.com

Manufactures self-adhesive, removable wall decals in a variety of sizes, colors, and styles.

WallCandy Arts

www.wallcandyarts.com

Manufactures self-adhesive, removable wall decals in a variety of sizes, colors, and styles.

glossary

Accent: A feature that gives a distinctive visual emphasis to something.

Accent Lighting: A type of lighting that highlights an area or object to emphasize that aspect of a room's character.

Aromatherapy: A form of alternative medicine that uses essential oils to positively affect a person's mood or health.

Blinds: A window covering with horizontal or vertical slats that can be compacted to reveal the window. The slats are often adjustable to admit light.

Box Spring: An upholstered bedspring made of a number of spiraled springs, each in a cloth pocket.

Café Curtain: A short curtain that covers only the upper or lower portion of a window.

Carbon Footprint: The amount of carbon dioxide produced by a person, organization, or location.

Cleat: A two-pronged piece of wood or metal around which a cord can be wrapped and secured.

Consignment: Property sent to an agent for sale; the consignor retains ownership until the item is sold, and then receives the payment minus the agent's fee.

Contemporary: Any modern design (after 1920) that does not contain traditional elements.

Convertible Sofa: A sofa that contains a mattress, which folds out to create a bed suitable for two people when necessary.

Daybed: A bed made up to appear as a sofa. It usually has a frame that consists of a headboard, a footboard, and a sideboard along the back.

Decoupage: The technique of decorating something using pieces of paper, fabric, or other flat materials, over which varnish or lacquer is applied.

Distressed Finish: A decorative-paint technique in which the final paint coat is sanded and battered to produce and aged appearance.

Double Exposure: Two photographic images on the same piece of film, producing ghost images.

Downsize: To reduce the number of possessions within a home, ultimately to the essentials.

Eclectic: Design consisting of a combination of various styles and sources.

Eco-friendly: Not harmful to the environment.

Enzyme: Proteins produced by living organisms that produce a chemical reaction.

Ethnic: Characteristic of a particular culture, region, or people.

Faux Finish: A decorative-paint technique that imitates a pattern found in nature.

glossary

Flea Market: A market—usually outdoors—where inexpensive or secondhand items are sold.

Focal Point: The dominant element in a room or design, usually the first to catch your eye.

Freecycle: To participate in the Freecycle Network's online registry, which provides a forum for offering and receiving items for reuse or recycling. (See Gift Economy.)

Furring Strip: A strip used to provide a level surface for attaching wallboard.

Futon: A thin, flat bed consisting of cotton batting, which makes it pliable enough for the bed to fold. It can be used on the floor, as in Japanese custom, or more commonly, as part of a folding apparatus that converts from bed to sofa.

Gateleg Table: A drop-leaf table supported by a gate-like leg that folds or swings out.

Gel-flame fireplace: These fireplaces are safe and smokeless and burn an all-natural, jelled alcohol that is efficient and ecologically safe.

Gift Economy: A society where concurrent or recurring giving serves to redistribute valuables within the community and keep waste from accruing.

Heirloom: A possession handed down within a family from generation to generation.

Indirect Lighting: A more subdued type of lighting that is not head-on, but rather reflected against another surface, such as a ceiling.

Laminate: Consisting of or covered with thin layers, one over another.

Love Seat: A sofa-like piece of furniture that consists of seating for two.

Modular: Units of a standard size, such as pieces of a sofa, that can be fitted together.

Molding: An architectural band used to trim a line where materials join or create a linear decoration. It is typically made of wood, plaster, or a polymer.

Nest: To fit together, one within another.

Occasional Piece: A small piece of furniture for incidental use, such as end tables.

Ottoman: A low, cushioned seat without arms or a back.

Primary Color: Red, blue, or yellow that can't be produced in pigments by mixing other colors. Primaries plus black and white, in turn, combine to make all the other hues.

Refinish: To give a new surface to.

Refractory Table: A table with leaves at the ends, not in the center.

Repurpose: To use or change for use in another format.

Retro: A design reminiscent of things past.

Salvage: To save something from loss or destruction.

Secondary Color: A mix of two primaries; orange, green, and purple.

Sectional: Furniture made into separate pieces that coordinate with each other. The pieces can be arranged together as a large unit or independently.

Shabby Chic: A form of design where items are either chosen for their age and signs of wear or are purposely distressed to achieve that appearance.

Shade: A sheet of cloth or paper on a spring roller used as a window covering.

Sleeper Chair: Similar to a convertible sofa, a chair that contains a mattress and converts to a bed suitable for one person.

Slipcover: A fabric or plastic cover that can be draped or tailored to fit over a piece of furniture.

Sponge Finish: A decorative-paint technique in which paint is applied lightly to an already-painted surface using a sponge.

Tapestry: A woven cloth designed to hang on walls for decoration.

Task Lighting: Lighting that concentrates in specific areas for tasks, such as preparing food, applying makeup, reading, or doing crafts.

Tension Rod: A rod that can extend to a determined size.

Thrift Shop: A store that sells used items, especially clothing, to benefit a charitable organization.

Tieback: An item used for holding a curtain back to one side.

Trompe L'oeil: Literally meaning "fool the eye," it is a painted mural in which realistic images and the illusion of three-dimensional space are created.

Trundle Bed: A low bed on small wheels that is kept underneath a normal bed.

Underlayment: Material laid between a sub-floor and a finish floor.

Upcycle: The practice of using something disposable for a greater purpose.

Upholster: To provide furniture with padding, springs, webbing, and/or covers.

Vintage: Representing the best of a past time.

index

index

M

Machine-washable fabrics, 130
Magazines, storage of, 99
Mattresses, 104
Measuring tape, 11
Medicine cabinet, wall-mounted, 99
Memory boards, 113
    making, 114
Message boards, 113, 115
Message centers, 94
Metal frame beds, 101
Microwave, storage for, 107
Mind, keeping an open, 22
Mirrors, 74
    cleaning, 155
Modular furniture, 26
    in office, 110
    as wall units, 61
Moving, 140–159
    change of address kit, 141
    DIY, 144
    fast-find cartons in, 146
    fragile items in, 144
    getting to know neighborhood, 142
    keeping old phone books, 140
    labeling boxes in, 146
    packing in, 141

    packing materials in, 145
    pet arrangements and, 143
    planning in, 140, 141
    transportation in, 144
Moving company, finding, 144
Multitiered baskets, 100
Murals, wall, 41
Murphy beds, 101

N

Native American-inspired blankets, 43
Natural oils, 125
Natural remedies, 155
Neighborhood, getting to know, 142
Nesting, 29

O

Odor solutions, 154
Offices
    closets for, 111
    modular, 110
    wardrobes as hideaway, 87
Ottomans, 31
    sleeper, 28

P

Packing materials, 145
Paint
    fabric, 46
    getting discounted, 37
Paint effects, 37, 122
Painter's tape, 13
Painting, 150
Papers, storage of important, 80–81
Paper shades, 66
Partitions, 50
Pegboards, 115
Pets
    making arrangements for, in moving, 143
    odors from, 154
Phone books, keeping old, 140
Photos
    black and white, 48
    taking before, 11
Plastic laminate, stain removal from, 155
Platform beds, 101, 104
Pocket folders, 80
Possessions, sorting, 14

R

Recellular.com, 18
Refinishing, 121, 126
    crackle glaze in, 123

paint effects in, 122
Rental agreements, checking, 141
Resilient vinyl, 56
Runners, table, 70

S

Salvation Army, 19
Schools, 19
Screens
    fabric, 51
    folding, 50
Seating subes, 29
Sectionals, 26
Shades
    fabric honeycomb, 68
    paper, 66
Sheer curtains, 68
Shelves
    adding, in bedroom, 71
    adjustable, 98
Shoes, storage of, 83
Sketch, making a, 11
Sleeper chairs, 28
Sleeper ottoman, 28
Slipcovers, 130
Small spaces, 90–115
Sofas
    convertible, 27
    ordering replacement cushions for, 130
    slipcovers for, 130
    two-piece, L-shaped, 26
Soft goods for bedrooms, 71
Soft touches, adding, 70
Space, utilizing all available, 84
Spice racks, 64
Spray painting, 121
Stacked tables, 29
Stain removal, 155
Stain repellants, 130
Storage, 30
    of important papers, 80–81
    microwave, 107
    mounted, 99
    quick-access, 112
    of take-out menus, 64
    under-the-bed, 21, 103
    vertical, 83, 92, 95, 96
Storage chest, 23
Storage cubbies, 100
Study solutions, 109–115

T

Tables
    bench, 94
    bistro, 106
    console, 94
    fabric toppers for, 126
    multipurpose, 105
    scarves and runners for, 70
    shopping for, 105

stacked, 29
Take-out menus, storage of, 64
Television, wall-mounted shelves for, 95
Tension rods, 40
    choice of, 68
    in closet, 85
    sheer curtains on, 68
    sheets on, 68
3-D art, 44
3-D room design program, 12
Tie-backs, 69
Transportation, in moving, 144
Treasure hunting, 119
Trundle beds, 104
Trunks, 30

U

Under-the-bed storage units, 21, 103
Upcycling, 134–135
Upholstered furniture, stain removal from, 155
Upholstered headboards, 72–73
Utensils, displaying, 88–89

V

Vacuum-seal bags, 86
Valuables, storage of, 109
Vertical storage, 83, 92, 95, 96
Vinyl films for windows, 66
Viritual paint selection, 36

W

Walk-through, importance of making, 10–12
Wall
    applying fabric to, 39–44
    color of, 34–37
    graffiti on, 42
    murals on, 41
Wall art, creating, 45
Wall hangings, 34, 38
Wall pockets, 80
Wall repairs, making, 147–150
Walls, cleaning, 157
Wall units, modular, 61
Wardrobes, 87
White vinegar, 155
Window frames, 120
Windows
    frosting, 67
    getting light in, 66–68
    vinyl films for, 66
Wood conditioners, 125
Wood floors, 56
    fixes for, 151

Y

Yard sales, 119, 121

photo credits

Illustrations used throughout: (trunk, picture frame, coat rack, vases, floor lamp, and tea cup on books) Karen Wolcott; (chapter openers) Kathryn Wityk.

page 1: courtesy of IKEA **page 3:** courtesy of Armstrong **page 4:** courtesy of IKEA **page 6:** *top left* Maria Dryfhout/Dreamstime.com; *top right* courtesy of Hunter Douglas; *bottom* courtesy of IKEA **page 7:** *top* courtesy of IKEA; *bottom* Mehmet Dilsiz/Dreamstime.com **page 8:** courtesy of IKEA **page 10:** Rob Parham Photography **page 11:** *top both* Vincent Alessi; *bottom* Dennis Workman/Dreamstime.com **page 12:** *both* Lixai/Dreamstime.com **page 13:** courtesy of IKEA **page 14:** Plasticrobot/Dreamstime.com **page 15:** courtesy of IKEA **page 16:** Maureen Plainfield/Dreamstime.com **page 17:** Chris Everard/Narratives **page 18:** courtesy of Ballard Designs, Inc. **page 19:** Jennifer Calvert/CH **page 20:** courtesy of IKEA **page 21:** courtesy of Forbo **pages 22–23:** *left* courtesy of Viva Terra; *right* courtesy of IKEA **page 24:** courtesy of EZ Moves **page 25:** Claire Richardson/Narratives **pages 26–29:** courtesy of IKEA **page 30:** Tony Giammarino/Giammarino & Dworkin, design: Christine McCabe; *inset:* courtesy of Viva Terra **pages 31–34:** courtesy of IKEA **page 35:** Ngoc Minh Ngo, design: Rob Southern **page 36:** courtesy of Glidden **page 37:** courtesy of Sherwin Williams **page 38:** courtesy of IKEA **page 39:** *top* Niklas Ramberg/ Dreamstime.com; *bottom* John Puleio/CH **page 40:** *top* Jan Baldwin/Narratives; *bottom* courtesy of IKEA **page 41:** Mark Samu **page 42:** courtesy of IKEA **pages 43–44:** courtesy of Viva Terra **pages 45–46:** courtesy of IKEA **page 47:** Vincent Alessi **pages 48–49:** *left* courtesy of Command/3M; *right* courtesy of IKEA **page 50:** courtesy of Wood-Mode **page 51:** Kate Gadsby/Narratives **page 53:** Eric Roth **page 54:** Bob Greenspan, stylist: Susan Andrews **page 56:** *top* courtesy of Armstrong; *bottom* courtesy of IKEA **page 57:** courtesy of Forbo **page 58:** courtesy of Armstrong **page 59:** *top* Freeze Frame Studio/CH; *bottom* row courtesy of Armstrong **page 60:** courtesy of InterfaceFLOR **page 61:** *top* courtesy of Ballard Designs, Inc.; *bottom* courtesy of Merillat **pages 62–64:** *all* courtesy of Ballard Designs, Inc. **page 65:** courtesy of Viva Terra **page 66:** courtesy of Hunter Douglas **page 67:** *both* courtesy of Rust-Oleum **page 68:** *top* courtesy of Hunter Douglas, *bottom* courtesy of IKEA **page 69:** *all* John Parsekian/CH **page 70:** *left* Maria Dryfhout/Dreamstime.com; *right* courtesy of IKEA **page 71:** courtesy of IKEA **page 73:** courtesy of Thibaut **page 74:** *top* courtesy of Viva Terra; *bottom* courtesy of IKEA **page 75:** *both* courtesy of IKEA **page 76:** courtesy of Viva Terra **pages 77–78:** *all* courtesy of IKEA **page 79:** *left* Eric Roth; *right* Stanistaw Kostrakiewicz/Dreamstime.com **pages 80–81:** *all* courtesy of Ballard Designs, Inc. **page 82:** courtesy of IKEA **page 83:** *top* courtesy of Organize-it; *bottom* courtesy of ClosetMaid **pages 84–85:** *left* courtesy of IKEA; center Bruce McCandless; *right* courtesy of ORG **page 86:** *left*

Travis Manley/Dreamstime.com; *right* Georgii Dolgykh/Dreamstime.com **page 87:** *left* courtesy of IKEA; *right* courtesy of Merillat **pages 88–92:** *all* courtesy of IKEA **page 93:** *both* courtesy of Improvements Catalog **page 94:** courtesy of Ballard Designs, Inc. **page 95:** Tatjana Strelkova/Dreamstime.com **page 96:** Jan Baldwin/Narratives **page 98:** courtesy of IKEA **page 99:** *top* courtesy of Viva Terra; *bottom* courtesy of Designer Rods **pages 100–101:** *all* courtesy of IKEA **page 102:** *both* courtesy of ORG **pages 103–106:** *all* courtesy of IKEA **page 107:** courtesy of Merillat **page 108:** courtesy of Improvements Catalog **pages 109–110:** *all* courtesy of IKEA **page 111:** Tony Giammarino/Giammarino & Dworkin **pages 112–113:** courtesy of Ballard Designs **page 114:** Casejustin/Dreamstime.com, *insets: top left* Jennifer Calvert; *right* courtesy of Thibaut; *bottom left* courtesy of Viva Terra **page 115:** *top* courtesy of Ballard Designs, Inc.; *bottom* Sandra Cunningham/Dreamstime.com, *inset: right* courtesy of IKEA **page 116:** courtesy of Ballard Designs, Inc. **page 118:** courtesy of Ballard Designs, Inc. **page 119:** Polly Eltes/Narratives **page 120:** Jan Baldwin/Narratives **page 121:** Ryan Newton/Dreamstime.com **page 122:** Mehmet Dilsiz/Dreamstime.com **page 123:** Rich Yasick/Dreamstime.com **page 124:** Jan Baldwin/Narratives, *inset:* Vvvstep/Dreamstime.com **page 125:** *top* George Ross/CH; *bottom* Picamaniac/Dreamstime.com **page 126:** Sebastian Czapnik/Dreamstime.com **page 127:** *clockwise* Claudiodivizia/Dreamstime.com; Ricardo Alday/Dreamstime.com; courtesy of Expanko; courtesy of Expanko; Ariusz Nawrocki/Dreamstime.com; courtesy of Expanko **page 128:** *left* Hunk/Dreamstime.com; *right* courtesy of IKEA **pages 129–131:** courtesy of IKEA **page 132:** *left* Valpal/Dreamstime.com; *right* Mark Huls/Dreamstime.com **page 133:** Andy Ryan/CH **page 134:** Felinda/Dreamstime.com **page 135:** Viktor Prokopenya/Dreamstime.com **page 136:** *top* allenangel/Dreamstime.com; *bottom* Kirill Vorobyev/Dreamstime.com **page 137:** courtesy of Viva Terra **page 138:** courtesy of Ballard Designs, Inc. **pages 140–141:** James Nemec/Dreamstime.com **page 142:** Kenneth Sponsler/Dreamstime.com **page 143:** Jennifer Walz/Dreamstime.com **page 144:** Claire Richardson/Narratives **page 145:** Jan Baldwin/Narratives **page 146:** Brad Calkins/Dreamstime.com **pages 147–149:** *all* John Parsekian/CH **page 150:** Norman Pogson/Dreamstime.com **page 151:** courtesy of Armstrong **pages 152–153:** *all* courtesy of Shaw **page 154:** Tzooka/Dreamstime.com **page 155:** Elena Ray/Dreamstime.com **page 156:** courtesy of IKEA **page 158:** Sam Aronov/Dreamstime.com, *inset:* Dmitry Kutlayev/Dreamstime.com **page 159:** *top* Franz Pfluegl/Dreamstime.com; *bottom* Suzanne Tucker/Dreamstime.com **page 161:** courtesy of Ballard Designs, Inc. **page 162:** courtesy of IKEA **page 165:** courtesy of IKEA **page 166** courtesy of Viva Terra **page 175:** courtesy of IKEA

Have a home decorating project?

Look for these and other fine

Creative Homeowner books

wherever books are sold.

300 color photos. 304 pp.; 7" × 9¼"
$19.95 (US) $21.95 (CAN)
BOOK #: 279659

500 color photos. 320 pp.; 8½" × 10⅞"
$24.95 (US) $27.95 (CAN)
BOOK #: 279323

275 color photos. 224 pp.; 9¼" × 10⅞"
$21.95 (US) $23.95 (CAN)
BOOK #: 279031

400 color photos. 304 pp.; 9¼" × 10⅞"
$24.95 (US) $29.95 (CAN)
BOOK #: 279679

For more information and to order directly, go to
www.creativehomeowner.com